What
Sign Is
Your Pet?

What Sign Is Your Pet?

BY DR. DONALD WOLF

TAYLOR PUBLISHING COMPANY
Dallas, Texas

Copyright © 1989 by Donald Wolf

Published by
Taylor Publishing Company
1550 West Mockingbird Lane
Dallas, Texas 75235

DESIGNED BY LURELLE CHEVERIE
ILLUSTRATIONS BY HERB MOORE

Library of Congress Cataloging-in-Publication Data

Wolf, Donald.
What sign is your pet? / Donald Wolf.
         p.   cm.
     ISBN 0-87833-681-8
1. Astrology and pets.   I. Title.
   BF1728.3.W65   1989   89-30440
   133.5'86360887—dc20   CIP

Printed in the United States of America

10 9 8 7 6 5 4 3 2 1

To Pepper, Doc, Happy, Kitty,
Squirt, and Bongo —
Happy trails,
until we meet again.

Acknowledgments

I wish to thank Joan Larsen for typing the final draft and Anne Matthews for her editorial assistance.

Thanks also to the many authors, too numerous to mention, whose pioneering publications on astrology served as the foundation for my early studies in this field.

I greatly appreciate the moral support I received from my family, my friends, and especially my wife, Shelly.

Finally, I want to thank all my clients and patients, who served as the inspiration for this book.

Contents

Introduction

There is a growing awareness among people on this planet that we are not alone. We share our earthly boundaries with other living, thinking creatures. These other living, thinking biological systems are subjected to the same environmental and cosmic influences as the human race.

Science is ever-changing. Many "old wives' tales" become proven scientific facts, and just as many accepted scientific facts are disproven and discarded. Recent advances in technology (and ways of thinking) have shown there is much intelligence and communication within the animal kingdom — more than we ever imagined.

The cosmos influences behavior in animals just as it does in humans. Based upon my recorded observations for over a decade as a veterinarian, as well as before my professional career, I have categorized the behavioral traits and quirks of animals into the twelve signs of the zodiac. I have used the data from over ten thousand former dog and cat patients in my own private practice, my astrological studies, and the aid of a computer to compile this book.

I personally experienced, at an early age, the direct effects of the stars on animals. I began to raise and train racing homing pigeons at the age of fourteen. There were certain times of the year when many of my best birds would not return home for days, or even become permanently lost. Other pigeon flyers had the same coincidental experience. The weather would be perfect, with no obvious reason for the high losses of our homing pigeons. Many "oldtimers," whose families had raced pigeons in Belgium for generations, said it was caused by the sun, with no further explanation.

A little investigation and record-keeping was enlightening. I soon correlated these unusual losses to days when the sun, our closest and most influential star, was most active with sunspots. The relationship was obvious and has since been proven. Sunspots affect the earth's magnetic field, which homing pigeons use for navigation. Knowledgeable pigeon flyers now anticipate heavy losses on days when there are lots of sunspots.

Behavior among even pure breeds of dogs or cats is never consistent. Not all pit bulls are aggressive. Not all poodles make huggable lap dogs. Even subsequent litters of pups and kittens from the same parents may not behave the same. My receptionist and technicians would often remark, "There sure are a lot of hyper pups and kittens this month (Aries and Gemini born)." At other times of the year

1

they would comment, "Why can't all the pups and kittens be like the mellow ones we've seen lately? (Capricorn, Pisces and others)." Pet personalities cannot be accurately predicted by bloodline alone. If the birth dates and behavior of these animals are closely studied, many of the differences in personalities are explainable astrologically.

By thoroughly understanding what makes each animal "tick," owners are better able to form a more compatible and humane relationship with their pet. Knowledge of their pet's inherent astrological traits enhances co-living, co-learning, and strengthens the animal-human bond.

So — what sign is *your* pet?

1

Determining When Your Pet Was Born

Usually a call to your pet's veterinarian will give you the age your pet was when you first went in for puppy or kitten vaccinations. Up to six months of age, pups and kittens are easily and accurately aged by qualified veterinarians. Simple deduction on your part can then identify your pet's birthdate.

If you acquired your pet when it was young but did not visit a veterinarian, you can still calculate its age when you took it home. Most puppies are acquired from six to nine weeks of age. Most kittens are acquired from five to eight weeks of age. Five- to six-week-old puppies and kittens are very infantile, requiring much care. Supplemental heat, much crying and whining, and lots of handling by the new owners is the norm. One key is that pups and kittens at this young age seem to urinate every time you take them out of the box. They may even urinate in their sleeping quarters. Their locomotor skills are just beginning to develop, so they are clumsy and fall a lot. Usually unable to hop up stairs or climb, they play and explore very little.

Puppies and kittens in the eight- to nine-week category have more control over their bladders, and can hold themselves until you take them to the litter box or outdoors. They rarely will urinate in their box if kept in one at night. They can walk very well, jump, hop up stairs, and climb. Playfulness and curiosity are beginning to develop.

If your pet was not a pup or kitten when you acquired it, or you can't remember when it came into your household, refer to the checklist and test to determine its astrological sign.

3

Checklist —
WHAT SIGN IS YOUR PET?

If Your Pet:
- is energetic, active, restless
- is friendly and cheerful, never depressed
- loves to be the center of attention
- likes noisy crowds of people or animals
- has a quick temper but it doesn't last
- pulls you for walks at the end of the leash
- is not vicious
- has a low threshold of pain (difficult for your vet to give injections to)
- trusts humans
- has fine but straight bone structure
- is wide chested
- stands as if at a show
- has an arched nose with crooked teeth or an overbite

Then Your Pet Is Probably: ARIES

If Your Pet:
- is quiet and calm
- is well behaved and obedient
- is slow and cautious in movement, not wasting any energy
- doesn't roam
- has a big appetite, sleeps a lot in one spot and is not easily disturbed
- has a high threshold of pain
- is very strong but gentle
- has a deep, larger than life voice
- is possessive of toys and overprotective and fond of children
- prefers the outdoors (lazing around)
- has thick bones, thick fur, and a thick build
- is medium height with clean, curly or wiry fur compared to similar animals

Then Your Pet Is Probably: TAURUS ✓

4

If Your Pet:

- is high spirited, even frantic at times
- is full of nervous energy
- loves to travel, escape, roam
- doesn't like to be alone
- likes to bark, meow, growl or hiss a lot
- could take or leave toys
- is easily injured
- would rather run than walk somewhere
- changes personalities with different people
- is tall and slender for its breed
- has lean musculature
- is colored or marked differently on one side of its body from the other

Then Your Pet Is Probably: GEMINI

If Your Pet:

- is calm and quiet
- is a homebody, except to go out swimming
- rarely or never gets into fights
- has a fear of strange people or animals
- is very gentle with children, pups, kittens, and their toys
- doesn't like to take car rides or go visiting
- is possessive of toys, food, etc.
- is afraid of loud noises
- has a spot on fur shaped like the moon
- was an abandoned orphan
- has short legs and a large head
- has small but even and healthy teeth
- has smooth and silky fur for its breed

Then Your Pet Is Probably: CANCER

If Your Pet:

- is strong but controls its strength
- loves to explore new places
- is calm, steady and graceful
- is devoted to family members

5

- has a strong tendency to roam
- acquires a following of animals when out
- is very protective of animal friends as well as family members, overprotective of kids
- develops strong bonds to children
- is the leader of a pack of animal friends
- likes water
- has a strong, bony frame with firm muscles
- has a very strong-looking jaw
- has a smooth stalking gait

Then Your Pet Is Probably: LEO

If Your Pet:

- is timid and shy
- is gentle
- is uneasy around and avoids newcomers
- is sympathetic and compassionate to the sick or handicapped
- gets frequent digestive tract upsets
- is very finicky and eats only small portions
- is easy to train, does all kinds of tricks
- is very quiet
- prefers a clean environment and cleans self constantly
- copies other animals
- is fascinated with even the tiniest of creatures
- is petite but well proportioned
- is lean and attractive (perhaps with green eyes)

Then Your Pet Is Probably: VIRGO

If Your Pet:

- leaves when voices are raised
- is a glutton for all types and amounts of food
- is everybody's pet
- is gentle and couldn't scare a flea
- is not a good watchdog or protector
- is sometimes stubborn and unresponsive
- is easy to fool, trick, or dupe
- needs family interaction, hates to be alone

- hates to be locked in a room, may develop claustrophobia
- has tendencies towards laziness
- doesn't roam or get into territorial fights
- enjoys mild climates best, dislikes hot or cold days
- is tall and slim
- has a long head and neck
- has a rough coat for breed

Then Your Pet Is Probably: LIBRA

If Your Pet:

- is round and ready
- is aggressive and fights frequently
- makes other animals frightened and uneasy
- is very possessive of belongings and territory
- is intensely loyal to one or two people
- has a very, very strong body and will
- has never killed another animal
- is a poor parent or has abandoned its young for no apparent reason
- remembers unkind acts
- is hard to train and not very obedient
- has an unusually strong desire to mate
- is heavily boned and medium to tall
- has a wide skull with thick jaw muscles
- has thick, dark fur

Then Your Pet Is Probably: SCORPIO

If Your Pet:

- travels and roams a lot, sometimes with other animals
- prefers being outdoors
- likes and is liked by children
- trusts people to extremes
- never seems to grow up emotionally
- is buddies with the neighbors and their pets
- has much stamina and energy when outdoors
- is difficult to train to do tricks
- brings other animals home

- may leave home for days at a time
- has a home-away-from-home to visit
- can take lots of kidding and abuse
- is very intelligent but often lacks common sense
- looks taller than it actually is
- has lean musculature
- has large but straight teeth
- has fine, light-colored fur

Then Your Pet Is Probably: SAGITTARIUS

If Your Pet:

- is easygoing
- rarely fights
- is slightly shy
- is easily depressed
- is coordinated and surefooted, never clumsy
- is a slow learner but obedient/persevering
- craves and consumes unusual objects
- lives far beyond expectations or recovers from usually fatal illness
- can be trusted and left at home without any worry
- is content to walk at your side or behind you even without a leash
- barks or meows only for good reason
- never cried as a pup or kitten
- is long-bodied or long-legged
- is slender and small-boned
- has long, straight fur for the breed

Then Your Pet Is Probably: CAPRICORN

If Your Pet:

- likes the water and outdoors
- does not take commands willingly
- makes friends with other animals easily
- gets along in crowds of people or animals
- searches endlessly for lost/misplaced toys or possessions
- is very vocal (barks and meows for no reason) and even

makes sounds resembling words
- is so curious it gets in trouble
- inspects and sniffs all newcomers
- may be obedient but not for long
- does not like the cold
- is very playful, well-liked by children
- is unpredictable
- does not sleep in any one specific area in house, but often uses new areas
- is tall and awkward-looking
- has soft, straight fur
- has blue or gray eyes

Then Your Pet Is Probably: AQUARIUS

If Your Pet:

- is very gentle, even mellow
- is calm and tranquil
- rarely fights, and if losing is smart enough to quit before injured
- was very sickly when young
- is quiet with a soft voice
- prefers to spend time at home
- is compassionate to the sick and disabled
- doesn't develop routines (eats and goes outside at all different times)
- is indifferent to excitement going on around it
- likes the basement, cellar, and other dark places
- avoids mean people or mean animals
- can sense impending bad weather or disasters
- feels bad for long periods of time after being punished
- is short and small for breed
- has large, bulging eyes
- has small paws and small teeth
- moves around slowly and gracefully

Then Your Pet Is Probably: PISCES

If you're still not sure of your pet's sun sign,
take the *What Sign Is Your Pet?* Test on the next page.

The
What Sign Is Your Pet?
Test

Part 1.

Choose the general characteristic which best describes your pet from each numbered category. Place a check mark next to your choice on the line provided. If neither applies, leave category unchecked. Total all the letters that correspond to your selections in the space provided at the end. The total will be added to your selections from a second list of key indicator characteristics for your pet.

1. ACTIVE, RESTLESS, or ENERGETIC   A,A,C,F,H,I,K,K   ——

   CALM, QUIET, WELL BEHAVED   B,D,E,G,J,L,L   ——

2. PREFERS OUTDOORS   B,H,I,J   ——

   PREFERS INDOORS   D,D,G,L,L   ——

   EQUAL PREFERENCE FOR BOTH   A,C,F,K,E   ——

3. VERY VOCAL   C,C,H,K,K   ——
   (barks, meows, growls, hisses a lot)

   VERY QUIET   B,B,D,F,F,I,J,J,L,L   ——

   NEITHER VOCAL NOR QUIET   A,E   ——

4. OCCASIONALLY FIGHTS   A,B,E,F,I   ——

   ALWAYS FIGHTS   H,H   ——

   NEVER FIGHTS (unless provoked)   C,D,G,J,K,L   ——

5. VERY CAUTIOUS OF OR AVOIDS
   STRANGE PEOPLE AND ANIMALS   B,D,E,F,F,J,L,L   ——

   MINGLES WITH OR WILLINGLY
   APPROACHES STRANGE ANIMALS
   OR PEOPLE   A,C,G,G,H,I,K,K   ——

6. EASY TO TRAIN, USUALLY
   OBEDIENT   L,G,G,D,E,F,F,G,J,K,K   ——

   DIFFICULT TO TRAIN, USUALLY
   DISOBEDIENT   A,C,H,H,I,I   ——

7. HIGH THRESHOLD OF PAIN
   (takes vet injections well)   B,B,C,E,E,G,H,I,L   ——

   LOW THRESHOLD OF PAIN
   (resists vet injections)   A,A,D,F,J,K   ——

8. EVERYBODY'S PET   A,C,G,G,I,J,L,K   ___

    PET TO ONLY A SELECT FEW   B,D,E,F,H,H   ___

9. MOVES QUICKLY   A,C,C,F,I,K,K   ___

    MOVES SLOWLY   B,B,E,D,G,H,H,J,L,L   ___

10. ATTRACTED TO AND LIKES NOISY
    CROWDS OF PEOPLE OR ANIMALS   A,A,C,E,H,K,K   ___

    LEERY OF OR WITHDRAWS FROM
    NOISY CROWDS OF PEOPLE OR
    ANIMALS   B,D,F,G,G,I,J,L   ___

11. STRONG DESIRE TO TRAVEL (ROAM)   C,C,E,E,H,H,I,I   ___

    ROAMS OCCASIONALLY   A,J   ___

    PREFERS TO STAY HOME   B,D,D,F,G,G,K,L,L   ___

12. TENDENCY TOWARDS LAZINESS   B,D,E,J   ___

    NOT LAZY   A,C,F,G,H,I,K,L   ___

13. VERY POSSESSIVE AND
    PROTECTIVE OF TOYS, CHILDREN,
    AND/OR PREMISES   B,D,E,H,H   ___

    NOT OVERLY PROTECTIVE AND
    WILLING TO SHARE POSSESSIONS   A,C,F,G,G,I,J,K,L   ___

TOTALS: A ___   G ___

PART 1   B ___   H ___

             C ___   I ___

             D ___   J ___

             E ___   K ___

             F ___   L ___

Part 2.

Read over the following behavioral characteristics, then go back and select the best six (only six) which apply to your pet. Total the letters as you did in Part 1.

OFTEN CONSIDERED A "PEST" BY OTHER ADULTS, BUT CHILDREN LOVE IT	K,K	_____
OFTEN SICKLY AS PUP OR KITTEN	L,L	_____
LIVES WELL BEYOND NORMAL LIFE EXPECTANCY OR MAY HAVE RECOVERED FROM USUALLY TERMINAL DISEASE	J,J	_____
TRUSTS PEOPLE AND WILL EAGERLY HOP INTO A STRANGER'S CAR	I,K	_____
VERY POOR AS A PARENT AND MAY EVEN ABANDON ITS OWN YOUNG	H	_____
BECOMES HYPERACTIVE AND HARD TO CONTROL WHEN GROUPS OF PEOPLE VISIT	A,A,C,C	_____
HAS PATCH OF FUR OR SPOT SHAPED LIKE THE MOON	D,D	_____
AGGRESSIVE TOWARDS OTHER ANIMALS, WILL ATTACK OTHER ANIMALS, OR IS FRIGHTENED WHEN THEY ARE AROUND	H,H	_____
APPEARANCE AND BEHAVIOR DOESN'T CHANGE WITH AGE	J,J	_____
EASY TO TRICK OR DUPE	G,G	_____
DOESN'T MAKE ANY NEW ANIMAL OR PEOPLE FRIENDS AS IT AGES	H,H	_____
FASCINATED BY TINY CREATURES (INSECTS, BIRDS, BUTTERFLIES, ETC.)	F,F,K	_____
SEEKS OUT DARK PLACES (BASEMENTS, ATTICS, CELLARS)	L	_____

RESPONDS AND LISTENS TO ONE OR TWO PEOPLE ONLY	H	_____
SHORT MEMORY, FORGETS MANY THINGS PREVIOUSLY LEARNED	K,K	_____
BRINGS ANIMAL FRIENDS HOME AFTER OUT TRAVELING	I,I	_____
ATTRACTED TO SICK, HANDICAPPED, OR DISABLED ANIMALS AND PEOPLE	F,F,L,L	_____
STRONGLY PREFERS SAME SEX AS COMPANIONS	A,A	_____
STAYS VERY CALM WHEN EXCITEMENT IS GOING ON AROUND	L,L	_____
VERY SMART BUT AT TIMES LACKS COMMON SENSE	I,I	_____
SUREFOOTED AND COORDINATED, AVID CLIMBER AND/OR DIGGER	J,J	_____
VERY LARGE APPETITE WITH TENDENCIES TOWARDS OBESITY EVEN IF NOT NEUTERED	D,D,E,K,K	_____
LOVES WATER (EVEN IF PREFERS TO BE INDOORS)	D,D,E,K,K	_____
OFTEN CRAVES AND CONSUMES UNUSUAL OBJECTS	J,J	_____
DISLIKES GOING OUTSIDE ON EITHER VERY HOT OR VERY COLD DAYS	G,G,K,K	_____
VERY STRONG PHYSICALLY BUT RARELY FIGHTS, AND HAS NEVER BEEN INJURED	B,B,E,H	_____
LEADER OF THE PACK WHEN WITH OTHER ANIMALS	E,E,I	_____
DISLIKES ALL OTHER ANIMALS EXCEPT BABIES, PUPPIES, AND KITTENS	D,D,F,F	_____

FULL OF HIGH SPIRITED, FRANTIC, OFTEN UNCONTROLLABLE NERVOUS ENERGY	C,C,A,A,K	_____
EXPLORES EVERY NOOK AND CRANNY OF NEW AREA HYPERACTIVELY AND FRANTICALLY	C,C,E,K,K	_____
MUST LEAD WHEN WALKED ON LEASH (HARD TO HOLD BACK)	A,A	_____
PREFERS OPPOSITE SEX AS COMPANIONS	C,C	_____
IF OLD, ADORES YOUNG ANIMALS	A,A,D,D,E,F,K,K	_____
DEEP, LOUD VOICE LARGER THAN LIFE	B,B	_____
WILL DO ANYTHING TO ESCAPE AND TRAVEL (ROAM)	C,C,E,E,I,I	_____
FRAGILE PHYSIQUE, INJURIES COMMON	C,C	_____
VERY STRONG BODY WITH VERY, VERY STRONG TEMPERAMENT AND WILL	E,E,H,H	_____
DIGESTIVE TRACT UPSETS ARE FREQUENT BUT ALSO IS VERY FINICKY EATER	F,F	_____
ACCUMULATES ALL SORTS OF TOYS/BONES AND IS VERY POSSESSIVE AND PROTECTIVE OF THEM (WILL FIGHT OVER THESE OBJECTS)	B,B,D,H,H	_____
HAS DONE A HEROIC LIFESAVING DEED	E,E	_____
WILL COPY WHAT OTHER ANIMALS DO AND CAN PERFORM ALL SORTS OF TRICKS	F,F	_____
CAN SENSE IMPENDING BAD WEATHER OR DANGER	L,L	_____

14

KEEPS SELF EXTREMELY CLEAN
(WILL NOT USE LITTER BOX
UNLESS CLEAN)   F,F,L   _____

VERY SENSITIVE TO LOUD NOISES
(SENSITIVE EARS)   D,D,G,G,L,L   _____

HATES TO BE LEFT ALONE AT
HOME (MAY BECOME
DESTRUCTIVE), NOT A LONER   G,G   _____

BUDDIES WITH ALL THE
NEIGHBORS AND PETS, MAY HAVE
SECOND HOME OR BE CHILDREN'S
MASCOT   I,I,K,J   _____

TOTALS:	A	_____	G	_____
PART 2	B	_____	H	_____
	C	_____	I	_____
	D	_____	J	_____
	E	_____	K	_____
	F	_____	L	_____

Add totals of all letters from Part 1 and Part 2. The highest score is your pet's highest sign probability. The letters correspond to the following signs:

A = Aries   G = Libra
B = Taurus   H = Scorpio
C = Gemini   I = Sagittarius
D = Cancer   J = Capricorn
E = Leo   K = Aquarius
F = Virgo   L = Pisces

The
PET
Zodiac

2

Lively and Lionhearted:

The
ARIES
Pet

March 21 — April 19

The Aries Personality

Ruled by the planet Mars, Aries-born cats and dogs are bursting with energy. They're natural doers and leaders: active, courageous, independent, restless, and impulsive. Your quick-moving Aries can snatch a piece of food out of your hand in a flash, and will let you know in no uncertain terms when interested in dinner, going outside, or getting you out of a favorite chair. How you guide expressions of such vigorous high spirits is crucial to the happy development of the Aries character.

Aries pets love being the center of attention, and tend to think the world revolves around them. They believe that every object brought into the house is somehow for their exclusive use. If permitted, in fact, the Aries cat or dog can completely dominate the home. Be careful not to pamper them too much, and don't give in to every little demand. They are ruthless in taking advantage of indulgent owners, and will abuse your kindheartedness no end with the lighthearted egotism that marks the Aries animal.

On the other hand, you can always count on lots of action when the cheerful and friendly Aries pet is around. Enthusiastic Aries can easily wear out its welcome (and wear down your friends) in a remarkably short time. Shyness is never a problem with the Aries dog or cat; in fact, few people or animals have the sheer stamina to keep up with the hyperactive pace so characteristic of this sign. They love parties (the noisier the better) and mingle remarkably well with crowds of people or with groups of other animals. You can count on them to keep the group active — if, of course, they are allowed to be boss. A word to the wise: at times, the Aries pet's behavior can get a bit out of control, particularly when the pet is over-excited. You've been at parties where a pet dashes repeatedly through the crowd, eyes bright, tail up, looking for trouble? Chances are excellent that an Aries just went by. If you take your Aries pet visiting, it may well be reluctant to leave an especially lively gathering. Be firm.

While quick-tempered, the Aries pet is not vicious or cruel to other animals. If threatened, it will, however, fight its own battles. Rather than run and hide, the Aries animal will go out of its way to confront a known foe, preferring to charge rather than waiting for the enemy.

While Aries pets are fearless (perhaps too much so) in peer confrontations, they have a surprisingly low threshold for pain, and are among the least stoic members of the pet zodiac. Even the boldest Aries pets lose their nerve at the sight of the veterinarian's needle.

On the other hand, Aries pets are among the most trusting of sun signs. They invariably make the first friendly overtures, so be sure that everyone is glad to see them — after all, *they're* certainly glad to see *everyone*. Only repeated rejection, even abuse (verbal or physical), will induce the naturally sociable, extroverted Aries to shy away from human company.

Aries-born pets, in short, do not care for the role of second-class citizens, nor do they keep their feelings on the matter secret. You will be surprised (perhaps even horrified) when you find out how many people have heard of your Aries pet's exploits. Their reputation for innocent aggressiveness is well-deserved.

The Aries-born male pet gets along best with other males; the Aries female, with other females. When the Aries-born pet does get into a fight, it is usually with the opposite sex. Frankly, Aries behaves best when alone, without the temptations that company brings. If you're looking for an "only cat" or "only dog," Aries is your best bet.

However, an Aries puppy or kitten is one of the hardest for older pets to accept. The little one's rambunctious desire to take over can cause major dominance battles with the more senior pet, canine or feline. Giving an older Aries a new, younger companion may furnish *you* with a new lease on life, but bringing a young Aries to live with a mature pet of any sign won't please the old-timer at all.

On the bright side, Aries pets at all stages of life are seldom depressed, and *never* lazy. And they do tend to mellow with age. Don't give up on your little Aries firecracker: better days lie ahead. A mature Aries can be a delightful pet, curious, dignified, and alert. Meeting an elderly Aries, you'd never dream just how riotous a youth they look back on — unless, of course, you were there.

In training, remember first that the Aries pet is easily humiliated, and hates above all to be reprimanded in public — especially in front of its animal friends. However, an overt scolding does get the idea across, and the offending act probably will not be repeated soon.

Aries dogs and sometimes even Aries cats love to perform, especially if lavishly praised. Their impulsiveness and short attention spans make an extensive repertoire of tricks a real achievement, so you'd better stick with showy, one-time performances like rolling over, shaking hands, fetching, or bouncing a balloon. Leave the patient searching-out of hidden objects to the persistent Taurus pet, and acrobatic Frisbee-catching to the ambitious Leos and wild-and-crazy Sagittarians.

For a job well done, treat your Aries to the spicy, crunchy foods this sign craves: strong-flavored animal chows, bits of strong, salty cheddar cheese, or, better yet, nachos, and remember to share a piece or two of your barbecued beef and chicken as well.

Perhaps the greatest challenge faced by the owner of an Aries dog is training it to the lead. (Don't even *try* this with an Aries cat. A Virgo, Libra, or Capricorn cat may walk with perfect dignity on a leash; the Aries will be in the shrubbery in a minute, and you with it.) The would-be trainer can look forward to a considerable workout as the Aries canine pulls with characteristic determination at the very end of the lead. Start training your Aries out of this embarrassing habit when it is still very young. A choke chain, and repeated commands to heel, are clearly required here.

The Aries Parent

Aries pets make consistently good parents, although they may be extremely physical, almost rough, with their young, and will not run back to check up on the little ones every time they complain. Once mature, Aries cats and dogs readily accept younger additions (pet or human) to the household, adopting the youngsters and showing a conscientious interest in the newcomers' upbringing.

The Young Aries

Newborn Aries cry constantly for attention. Their eyes and ears open earlier than those of others of their species, and they become mobile as soon as they are born, wiggling around to every corner of their nest. The typical litter of Aries young-sters is strong, healthy, and *very* active. When you take it home, the Aries puppy of kitten will have you giving it new water and food and letting it outside every five minutes — *if* you allow such domination.

Young Aries pets learn quickly and rarely forget. Often, they refuse to follow your initial commands. Be persistent. If an Aries does not learn to obey when young and impressionable, you may well end up with a four-footed bully on your hands. If an Aries is neglected or handled cruelly while young, it may easily become destructive or downright vicious. It is especially important not to let a mean streak develop while raising Aries-born cats or dogs. They have long and accurate memories, and tend to generalize grudges. For this reason, Aries animals are not the best candidates for rehabilitation if taken into a home after having been abused, abandoned, or feral. A long, careful period (up to three or four years) of earning their trust is usually required.

The Healthy Aries

Most Aries-born pets possess a fine, straight bone structure and broad stance. Aries noses are often strongly arched, and crooked teeth or an overbite frequently occurs. Like Scorpio pets, Aries animals often have reddish fur, and are attracted to red objects. A red throw-pillow or rug of their very own will please them immensely.

Aries cats and dogs are particularly prone to problems of the nervous system. Seizures (usually controllable) are often seen in Aries veterinary patients. If your Aries pet has ever been knocked on the head hard enough to pass out, be particularly alert for possible mild seizures developing later in life.

Aries pets are also susceptible to kidney problems. Infections of the kidneys and chronic nephritis (the degeneration of the kidneys in old age) are typical complaints. So are blockages of urine flow, which may require surgery.

Aries skins are sensitive as well. Ringworm can be a problem in pets born under this sign, as can staph/bacterial infections in Aries puppies and kittens.

Otherwise, the only weak spot in the sturdy Aries system can be your pet's teeth and gums. Infections and abscesses are common (due, often, to the Aries tendency toward poor tooth configuration). Making sure the pet's teeth are cleaned regularly is a good idea.

Aries Summary

If you are looking for a calm, quiet pet for your home, Aries is not for you. If you want a happy, friendly, exuberant addition to the household, you have made the right choice. Remember: Aries pets need the room and opportunity to burn up energetic calories, but they mellow with age and willingly accept new pet additions to the family.

Aries Compatibilities

Aries pets get along well with most of the other animal sun sings. They bring a high level of enthusiastic energy to their relationships.

The best animal signs for Aries pets to share their home with are Aries, Gemini, Leo, Sagittarius, and Capricorn.

Animals with the sun signs of Taurus, Cancer, Virgo, Libra, Scorpio, and Aquarius make good friends with Aries pets on an occasional basis.

The only sun sign which Aries pets cannot seem to inspire is Pisces.

Aries Pets — Aries Pets

Animals with the sun sign of Aries like each other. They complement each other's personalities and will stay together most of the time, relieving their owners of constant involvement in their activities. Aries pets will play with each other to the point of exhaustion. Each will try to dominate the other, although they never resolve the question of who is boss. Tempers flare quickly with this pair, but the skirmishes are rarely serious.

Aries Pets — Taurus Pets

This is one of the few Aries combinations in which there will be little activity between the two. Taurus pets tend to ignore Aries pets' advances. Taurus does not relish the idea of expending the energy necessary to satisfy Aries. Aries pets will constantly try to stimulate Taurus pets to action, but Taurus becomes stubborn and won't budge. Taurus will become aggravated at Aries' disruptions of the peaceful quiet moments which are essential to Taurus's wellbeing.

Aries Pets — Gemini Pets

This is a very lively pairing and entertaining to be around. The nervous energy of Gemini pets, combined with the impulsiveness and rambunctiousness of Aries pets, makes for few quiet moments between the two. Gemini knows when to excite Aries to full tilt, all-out action, and also when to play gently. Aries pets are attracted to Gemini pets. Their owners may think that their Aries pet has taken off to engage in battle with one of their enemies, but if a Gemini pet is at the end of an Aries charge, the result will be nothing more than vigorous play. These two signs will tire each other out, although Gemini usually outlasts Aries in the energy department. Aries pets and Gemini pets get into a lot of mischief-making predicaments with each other.

Aries Pets — Cancer Pets

This pair will not be themselves if they are together constantly in the same home. The relationship is best kept infrequent. Timid and reserved Cancer pets will not give in to Aries pets' advances. Aries tries to dominate Cancer, but Cancer will never allow this to happen. Cancers become jealous when their owners show affection to Aries and will refuse to share their food, toys, or space with Aries. Aries pets are in for a violent surprise when they invade a Cancer pet's home.

Aries Pets — Leo Pets

Another exciting combination of animal signs is Aries and Leo, especially when Leo is feline and Aries is canine. The two will get along very well in the same home, each respecting the other's territory and possessions. This is a fun-loving pair and fighting is rare. Aries pets are good for Leo pets in that they liven up depressed Leos and have a quieting influence over the Leo's desire to be dominant.

Aries Pets — Virgo Pets

Aries-born pets are too aggressive for timid Virgos. The high-strung nature of Aries will totally dominate Virgo. Aries is attracted to the quiet Virgo and will enthusiastically go out of its way to aggressively greet the withdrawn Virgo. The Virgo pet will try to accommodate Aries, but lacks the stamina of the Aries and is eventually bossed around. Meetings between Virgo and Aries pets should therefore be kept short. Constant proximity will lead to a one-sided, Aries-dominated relationship.

Aries Pets — Libra Pets

Libra pets are better accepted by Aries pets if they are young puppies or kittens. Libras love to play with enthusiastic Aries. Aries feels the need to dominate Libra. Aries has to be first to get the handout from the table, first to be petted upon your return home, and first out the door when both are let outside. Libra and Aries pets occasionally irritate each other, but not to the extent of harmful fighting. For the most part, they get along if the companionship isn't permanent.

Aries Pets — Scorpio Pets

Aries pets know how to handle the strong Scorpio pet. Aries' fearlessness offsets the physical advantage of most Scorpios. This relationship is always active and energetic, with occasional eruptions of temper on both sides. Aries pets have a small edge in domination over Scorpio pets. Aries and Scorpio need to be separated for periods of time or they get in each other's way and fight.

Aries Pets — Sagittarius Pets

Sagittarius pets will get their own way with Aries pets, but they will not dominate Aries physically. Aries loves to play tricks on Sagittarius, often "hide and sneak." Aries and Sagittarius will share a lot of traveling adventures together. They always want to go outside and are difficult to keep indoors or at home. If you should take Aries and Sagittarius on vacation or visiting with you, they may disappear for hours. Aries and Sagittarius have endless fun with one another.

Aries Pets — Capricorn Pets

This is a happy, playful, and entertaining pairing of animal signs. The high-spirited Aries pet will initiate most of the activities. Capricorn is willing to join in the playfulness to the finish. Aries tends to dominate the relationship, but Capricorn is happy and emotionally stable. When Capricorn tries to initiate play, Aries is stubborn and may not start playing until it appears Capricorn has given up. Aries can be a bit snappy with Capricorn, but it rarely leads to fighting. Capricorn and Aries pets blend best when there are two dogs or two cats in the relationship. Aries dogs and Capricorn cats do not mix very well. Snapping and playing may lead to fighting between these different species.

Aries Pets — Aquarius Pets

When these two sun signs first meet they won't get along at all, but after two or three encounters they become good friends. The relationship eventually becomes energetic and intense. Aquarius pets will lead the way, teaching the Aries all sorts of strange behavioral traits. Aquarius will often abandon Aries when the two are off somewhere together, and Aquarius will come trotting home apparently pleased to have ditched Aries somewhere. Aquarius pets need time alone, and therefore do not do as well in the relationship if they are forcibly housed with Aries.

Aries Pets — Pisces Pets

Pisces does not think much of the energetic Aries. Aries pets are too forward and physical in their advances. Aries will be jubilant, bounding, and enthusiastic in greeting Pisces, but this rubs Pisces pets the wrong way. Pisces never gives in and this will cause the usually active Aries to become depressed and quiet. Occasionally Aries pets keep trying to stimulate Pisces pets to action and this results in the violent flaring of tempers.

3

Tranquil, Do Not Disturb:

The
TAURUS
Pet

April 20 — May 20

The Taurus Personality

The congenial Taurus pet, ruled by the planet Venus, is the most amiable personality in the zodiac. Quiet, well behaved and obedient, almost passive, Taurus pets feel no need to dominate. Other animals may skirmish wildly around them, but Taurus-born pets will simply sit and watch. Owners who single out the reticent Taurean cat or dog for a special pat or extra treat are rewarded ten times over with steady affection and unswerving loyalty.

Taurus-born pets like to pick their fights — and win their battles. Taurean counterattacks won't stop until the opposition is exhausted. It takes plenty of teasing, even provocation, from people or other animals before the Taurus pet erupts into rage. Once that anger is aimed, though, you'd best get out of the way! Remember: such outbursts are few and far between, and are *never* initiated by the Taurus pet.

Remember, too, that the Taurus disposition is both naturally kind and reinforced with a real sense of fair play. Cautious and even withdrawn when meeting new associates (human or animal), Taureans often have to be coaxed out from under the bed to greet newcomers, and will become unreservedly friendly with very few. But once they do, the attachment usually lasts for life. Even if the newfound pals aren't seen again for years, the Taurus pet will greet them affectionately when they reappear.

In the interim, many Taureans rely on their toys for a rewarding social life. Taurus pets are *very* possessive. They love to accumulate chew bones, balls, rolls of yarn, stuffed toys, old knotted socks, styrofoam packing material — you name it, a Taurus pet's surely got it. The security-blanket contentment they find in these collectibles dampens the latent temper in Taurus pets — to a point. (Don't try to separate pet and possessions unless you are prepared for some noisy consequences.)

Taurus pets instinctively like to have children in the home, and will guard a human child with enthusiasm. The only problem? Too much TLC on the part of the self-elected watchdog (or watch cat). Taurus pets can prove overprotective where pint-size *Homo sapiens* are concerned. But if, for any reason, you need a pet to protect your children, Taurus will prove more than up to the task.

The Taurus-born pet loves to lie around outdoors, and does best on farms or in the open suburbs. It's not that they need the running room — Taureans, unlike Aries pets, will never be accused of hyperactivity — but they do love a paws-to-the-earth, nose-to-the-wind life whenever possible. Given the choice, Taurus dogs and cats will spend the majority of their free time outdoors, rain or shine. They'll even willingly *sleep* outside when the weather is mild. (Otherwise, sensible Taurus holds out for a nice warm house and a nice warm bed... or, better yet, a place on the nearest electric blanket.)

Even on its best days, the Taurus pet moves around v-e-r-y slowly. These docile dogs and cautious cats know exactly where they're going, but take their own sweet time getting there. Taurus-spotting tip: they like to travel in a straight line from one spot to another — no detours, no second thoughts. Even other animals jumping against, on, around, or over true Taurus pets won't make them swerve from these point-to-point passages.

Perhaps because of their remarkable powers of concentration, Taurus-born pets are usually very obedient. Remember their slow nature, and give them plenty of time to respond to commands. They come when called, but at their own leisurely pace.

Not surprisingly, Taurus pets can take or leave traveling. Roaming behavior is uncharacteristic for these lovers of familiar territory, and car rides seem to rank right up there with baths and exercise as Most Unpopular Taurus Activities. If they know you want to go somewhere in the car, convincing Taurus pets to come along will surely cause delays. (There's one exception. Mention the name of one of your Taurus dog's few fast friends — "Let's go see Susie!" or "Let's go see Grandpa!" — and just watch them race you to the car. Don't bother to try this one on Taurus cats; catlike, they prefer to let friends come to *them*.)

The Taurus pet is quiet by nature. It will rarely bark, meow, or whine. When a Taurus cat or dog does vocalize, however, their voices tend to be deep, rich, and penetrating. Visitors who hear your Taurus pets before they see them will always remark that your pets "sounded much bigger."

The arrival of a Taurus pet often coincides with rapidly rising food bills. Yes, Taurus pets have voracious appetites. In fact, they hover over their food like vultures, chewing slowly, but always with room for more. Very often, they'll actually lie down while eating, like Roman emperors at a banquet.

Jealousy is simply not in Taurus pets' emotional makeup. They don't become depressed if you share your time with other animals or children; they won't sulk around the house. However, Taurus pets do seem to need long periods of rest. They're not easily awakened, and can sleep through anything. They prefer to pick one particular spot for snoozing, to which they'll consistently return when they feel the sandman calling. If disturbed, they will not get up and leave in a huff like Scorpio, but will stoically roll over and continue snoring.

Training the young Taurus pet is easy. No food or treats are needed. All they want is to be hugged and petted — a lot. Use affection as their reward, and Taurus-born pets become very obedient very quickly.

However, Taureans clearly consider three a crowd. Training a Taurus pet is easier when no one else is around. They will clam up when there's an audience, or lots of action, around them. Since Taureans hate to be surprised by loud voices, soft tones on your part will get more response than shouting. Remember, too — Taurus types need to become accustomed to routine responses. If you change the pattern, they'll be upset, resentful, and confused.

The Taurus Parent

Taurus pets are good caregivers, and especially good at keeping gentle order through well-timed nips, nudges, and stern looks. They spend more hours than average with their offspring, making your job easy. The strong silent Taurus pet, in fact, is remarkably gentle and patient with the demanding little brood, and can be especially sympathetic with sick or injured youngsters, conscientiously providing special attention to their survival among healthier sibling-competitors.

The Young Taurus

Are you thinking of adding a newborn Taurus pet to your household? The young Taurus will provide you with more ups than downs. Just expect periodic loud outbursts when they don't get their way, and — if you play rough — a boisterous response.

Young Taurus pets respond to and return physical affection. They love to be picked up and cuddled, and will often fall asleep in your arms. Though not outwardly friendly to other animals, Taurus puppies and kittens attract four-footed company…sometimes because other animals think young Taurus pets are easy marks.

They are wrong. The growing Taurus youngster is surprisingly strong, as you can feel when playing with it. The least fragile of all the signs, sturdy little Taureans can withstand hair-raising incidents in the ongoing Animal Olympics — a tumble off the porch, a misjudged refrigerator leap — that would surely require a trip to the veterinarian for any other signs.

The Healthy Taurus

The physical tendencies of Taurus-born pets are oddly reminiscent of the bull which governs this sign. In both cats and dogs, "thickness" is the dominant quality — thick bones, thick fur, thick build. Usually of medium height for their breed, Taurus pets' unusually wide chests and well-defined musculature give them a strong appearance. Taurus-born pets like to keep themselves clean (although not to the point of fetishism, as is typical of Virgo), carefully grooming the abundant curly or wiry fur which covers their unusually tough skin. Taurus eyes are large, dark, and very round; their gait deliberate, slow, and steady. (Note that the natural colors of the sky and earth — light blues and browns — suit Taurus pets best.)

Like all members of the pet zodiac, Taureans are prone to very specific clusters of health problems. Hypothyroid conditions (i.e., underactive thyroid glands) occur frequently — one reason so many become lazy, overweight, and fond of warmth at all costs. Like that other common Taurus ailment, bladder and/or kidney infections, thyroid complaints respond well to a veterinarian's care. Taurus pets are no sissies, unlike highstrung Aries, Leo, or Capricorn. Given their high pain thresholds, a veterinarian usually feels at ease when poking a Taurus pet with a needle.

The reproductive tract is another vulnerable Taurus territory. Be alert to prostate infections in male Taurus pets, and infections and tumors affecting uterus and ovaries in Taurus females.

Taurus necks and legs are vulnerable as well. They're sturdy, remember, but not *that* sturdy — ruptured disks in neck or back and scrapes and cuts on the legs are classic Taurean traumas, particularly in the adult or geriatric cat or dog.

Most characteristic, however, is the "fat cat" syndrome. Obesity in Taurus-born pets, male and female, feline and canine, is the number-one health problem. After neutering, especially, many gain weight very quickly. If owners don't practice strict portion and diet control at feeding time, ballooning waistlines will almost certainly result.

Taurus Summary

Taurus is as calm as Aries is animated. If you want a sober, responsible, and gentle pet with enormous affection for children, Taurus is a fine choice. Just remember that Taurus cats and dogs thrive best in suburbs or countryside. They do need long periods of solitude or sleep to maintain that equable temperament — and, occasionally, they need a strict diet as well.

Taurus Compatibilities

Slow, tranquil Taurus pets do not have many conflicts with other animals. Their passive nature usually poses little threat, even to those influenced by the more aggressive sun signs.

Animals with the signs of Taurus, Leo, Virgo, Libra, Sagittarius, and Pisces do well as constant companions for the Taurus pet.

Gemini, Cancer, Scorpio, Capricorn, and Aries make better casual acquaintances than housemates.

Aquarius pets and Taurus pets go after each other tooth-and-nail and should be kept apart.

Taurus Pets — Taurus Pets

The relationship between two Taurus pets (cats, dogs, or the mix) will be peaceful and uneventful. The signs are compatible but make each other placid. They are naturally comfortable and content with each other's company. They will keep each other home and roaming behavior is rare. They are affectionate and will cuddle and lick each other in their tender moments, although at times they will be stubborn in reciprocating one another's loving advances.

Taurus Pets — Gemini Pets

Gemini pets are just too fast and excitable for slow Taurus pets to appreciate. Taurus will not join in with the frantic behavior exhibited by Gemini. Little fighting occurs, but there is competition for food, bones, toys, and their owner's affection. Gemini pets constantly attempt to play with Taurus pets, but their invitation is rebuffed more times than not.

Taurus Pets — Cancer Pets

This coupling of sun signs will create a very quiet atmosphere. Cancer pets and Taurus pets are delicate and gentle with each other. Cancer often takes the unusual role of protector over Taurus. Both of these signs love to stay home. Cancer pets will stay indoors, while Taurus pets prefer to lounge around outdoors. Taurus and Cancer will eat you out of house and home if you let them. They won't leave any food lying around one another, preferring to gobble it down themselves. There will be a tendency for obesity when Taurus and Cancer are housed together and compete for food.

Taurus Pets — Leo Pets

There is lots of noise when Taurus and Leo pets are together. The barking, snarling, and meowing does not usually lead to fighting. These two signs just make each other very vocal. They are usually harmless together, with Leo dominating and Taurus following along. Leo pets make Taurus pets become more active, and Taureans will give Leos the run of the house.

Taurus Pets — Virgo Pets

Taurus-born pets love all Virgo-born animals. The bond and friendship between these two is likely to be lifelong. They are comfortable and content in each other's company. Even a large Taurus dog will play tenderly with a Virgo kitten. Both Virgo and Taurus are cautious when meeting strangers, so they take comfort and security in each other. Taurus will not take advantage of the easily dominated Virgo. In each other's company, their personalities will be separate and distinct.

Taurus Pets — Libra Pets

There will be little activity between pets in your home if they have the sun signs of Libra and Taurus. They will get along well, in a melancholy way, but they won't stimulate each other to physical activity. In fact, there is a tendency towards laziness when these two animal signs are together. They will both be content to lie around the house and be pampered by their owners. This pet pairing may appear boring, but it is predictable and trustworthy, and will give you very few worries.

Taurus Pets — Scorpio Pets

Taurus pets and Scorpio pets stick together through thick and thin. They fight as much as they get along, but they stay beside one another. Taurus is very tolerant of Scorpio's temperament and some of this patience rubs off on Scorpio. Scorpio is bound to occasionally disrupt the usually good nature of Taurus. There are times when Scorpio pets won't let Taurus pets alone until they fight. The two signs often feud over bones and toys.

Taurus Pets — Sagittarius Pets

Taurus and Sagittarius pets get along with each other without causing too much commotion, although they don't interact or share many activities. Neither will restrict the other's personality; they live and let live. Taureans are content to watch Sagittarians' antics and will not follow them on their frequent excursions away from home. Taurus doesn't even try to keep up with Sagittarius and Sagittarius doesn't try to coax Taurus along.

Taurus Pets — Capricorn Pets

These two animal signs are stubborn with each other's advances when they first meet. It takes time and Capricorn holds out longer, but they eventually get along well. Neither will become wild or uncontrollable when the other is around. They will both listen to and follow their owner's commands. Capricorns will only try once to take away the Taureans' bones or toys. They both love to play with children, will not fight for their attention or affection, and are safe to have together around children.

Taurus Pets — Aquarius Pets

The often pesty Aquarius pet triggers Taurus's anger. Fights are frequent between these two opposing animal signs. When not fighting, they are indifferent to each other and will growl when the other comes near. The obedient Taurus pet and the often disobedient Aquarius pet rarely find any neutral turf. This is an explosive match.

Taurus Pets — Pisces Pets

Taurus pets bring Pisces pets to life, often more than quiet Taurus would like. Pisces is the initiator of the action that occurs between the two; Taurus rarely approaches Pisces. Pisces pets are lively with a Taurus in their presence. Taurus will try occasionally to interrupt the active little Pisces, but to no avail. Pisces resists Taurus's attempts at settling them down. There will be plenty of tender and calm moments between the two, and Taurus will cherish and dominate these intimacies.

Taurus Pets — Aries Pets

This is one of the few Aries combinations in which there will be little activity. Taurus tends to ignore the advances of Aries. Taurus does not relish the idea of expending the energy necessary to satisfy Aries pets. Aries will constantly try to stimulate Taurus to action, but Taurus will become stubborn and won't budge. Taurus pets will become aggravated at Aries pets' disruptions of the peace and quiet which are essential to Taurus's well-being.

4

Life in the Fast Lane:

The
GEMINI
Pet

May 21 — June 21

The Gemini Personality

Gemini pets, ruled by the planet Mercury, are high-spirited, fleet of foot, and intensely (even insatiably) friendly and curious. An understanding owner who tolerates the Gemini drive for new experiences and fresh information will be rewarded by nonstop entertainment, as these lively explorers find new worlds to conquer in the most unlikely ways.

Energy is the watchword here — *lots* of nervous energy which can make Gemini behavior seem almost frantic at times. Cats and dogs under the sign of the Twins are intrigued by everything. When visiting an area for the first time, Gemini pets will take rapid inventory, spending very little time in one spot before darting off to the next. Gemini pets can be difficult to control when their avid curiosity triggers this frenzied behavior, and once excited, they are hard to settle down. How to spot a Gemini? Gemini dogs very often race in circles and bark when excited; Gemini cats pace back and forth, meowing, when agitated.

Gemini pets will welcome strangers into their home with much physical affection, readily bouncing into the newcomer's lap to purr, tread, or lick their new friend's face. With groups of visitors, Geminis fly among the guests with glee, but may become confused trying to please everyone at once. They rarely develop favorites, preferring quantity over quality. Geminis are the actors of the pet zodiac, highly unpredictable in their human (and animal) interactions, and are not above behaving differently with different companions. Hypocritical? Not really. Geminis simply have naturally changeable, chameleon-like personalities, and seem to know immediately which facet of their nature will be most endearing to which audience.

Gemini pets excel at picking out animal lovers. This is a surprisingly diplomatic sign, for all its apparent scatterbrained tendencies — Geminis, for instance, will not ask to play if you are not in the mood. They love to be picked up and petted and scratched all over and are delicate in their responses. Always ready for action, Twins rarely play rough. A mean Gemini pet is a rarity.

Geminis can make excellent "only pets" — for about two hours. They're inventive at amusing themselves with elaborate solitary games, but when left alone too long they can become excessively restless and absurd situations sometimes result. The local fire department, for instance, may come to know your Gemini pet extremely well. The cat that cheerfully climbs a tree with no return route is probably a Gemini. So is the dog who jumps into the water off a steep bank — then is absolutely unable to climb out without *lots* of assistance. The Gemini pet takes many risks, but oddly enough the outcome is almost always lucky.

For all their surface self-sufficiency, Gemini pets won't stay by themselves if they can help it. Even fences don't always keep in these Houdinis of the animal kingdom. Only Sagittarius pets are more dedicated to unscheduled travel. Large Gemini dogs are notorious fence hoppers; little ones, notorious fence climbers. And Gemini cats have no trouble at all escaping through the smallest cracks. If your Gemini pet has flown the coop, look for the nearest crowd, human or furry. Chances are Gemini was simply in search of a party — or, better yet, an appreciative audience.

The Gemini-born pet would rather run than walk. These speedsters can keep up with the best. Gemini dogs, for instance, make excellent jogging partners. Many Gemini-born cats are especially deft with their paws, and learn to use their rear feet with special force at an early age. If the front claws only are removed on Gemini felines, most will promptly attack your best furniture with their strong back feet.

Why do Gemini pets wander more than others? Two reasons: the desire to explore and the equally strong desire to propagate their species. As a result, Gemini pets may well require neutering earlier than their companions in the pet zodiac, but will show little or no ill-effects (e.g., obesity) of the operation.

Geminis are often bored in suburbs or countryside, but they adore big city life with its crowds, noise, and action. They'll even do well in very small homes or cramped urban apartments provided the atmosphere is lively. Geminis love to go visiting and even enjoy moving, the more frequently the better. Surprises, new places, stimulation — Gemini craves it all. If you can arrange a strategic "observation post" for a Gemini cat or dog overlooking a busy street, nothing will please this sign more. Just don't lock them in a room for any length of time. A closed door makes Gemini surprisingly anxious. The Twins, more than most, will cry at the door to be let out; then moments later cry to be let in again. Give them the run of the house, even if it's a studio apartment, and all will be well. Gemini pets have extremely acute hearing and eyesight, and are always looking up, down, around, and off in the distance. When they spot something especially exciting, expect gregarious Geminis to fetch you right away.

Gemini pets like to bark and meow. Long periods of silence and inactivity are unusual. Gemini dogs and cats (who usually get along very well) will happily bark and meow to each other, apparently understanding what the other species is saying. Because they don't develop strong attachments to toys or people, Geminis won't become jealous or fight if you give one of their playthings to another animal that is visiting. They're also perfectly safe to have around groups of children.

Gemini pets almost always prefer the opposite sex. Male Gemini pets will visit with female houseguests at length before greeting the men in the room. It is considerably easier for a female person to train a male Gemini pet, and vice versa.

Affection, not treats, is the best Gemini training reward. You may, in fact, have trouble in finding any food that agrees with your Gemini. Many diets give them excessive, noticeable intestinal gas. When you find something that agrees with their digestive system, stick with it.

The Gemini Parent

As parents, Gemini pets give their offspring much more freedom than is really needed. They utterly lack the responsibility and early parental discipline essential to preventing youngsters from becoming wild, even uncontrollable. Gemini parents, instead, will play endlessly with the little band of outlaws they've fostered, and won't develop proper routines of feeding and cleansing the young. You may even have to remind congenitally flaky Gemini to nurse the young at regular intervals. Parenting chores, sad to say, will fall almost entirely to you. Some signs are transformed by the great task of mother or fatherhood, but Geminis don't get the message — ever.

The Young Gemini

Gemini puppies or kittens, not surprisingly, are friendly and inquisitive. Not at all shy, they'll play with anything or anyone, and usually come from large litters. Quick, jumpy, and blessed with exceptional reflexes, baby Geminis are easily bored, easily distracted, and hard to handle when excited. Training sessions must be kept short. Remember that they respond best to owners whose sex is the opposite of theirs. Voice commands work better with the Gemini pet than do hand signals. You don't have to worry about reprimanding your Gemini pets — if they have short attention spans, they're also notoriously unable to nurse a grudge.

The Healthy Gemini

Gemini pets have unusually fragile physiques, and can be injured easily through falls and rough play.

In appearance, Gemini pets are tall and slender, with fine, delicate bones. They often have large, sometimes crooked teeth, and their musculature is lean, even thin. Pale fur and blue or gray eyes often signal a Gemini. If spots or patches of color appear on Gemini pets, such markings will often cluster on one side of the body, giving Gemini pets two quite different appearances in profile. Blue, yellow, and orange are the best colors for Gemini pets.

Delicate Gemini is vulnerable to a variety of ailments, some minor, some serious. Their fragile bones mean an unusual number of skeletal-system problems, from arthritis of the hips (hip dysplasia) to joint stiffness in shoulders and knees, as well as a tendency to leg, jaw, and skull fractures. The touchy Gemini digestion brings recurring diarrheas, usually dietary, and recurring flatulence (try digestive enzyme supplements). Gemini skin is delicate, too; skin cancers in light-furred Gemini cats, as well as dermatitis of the nose — often due to too much sun — are not unusual. Diseases of the blood run strongly in Gemini medical histories, too, particularly immune-deficiency syndrome and an inability to fight off seemingly minor infections.

Gemini Summary

If you want an active, entertaining pet to share your busy life, Gemini will fit these needs beautifully. If your house resembles Grand Central Station, the Gemini-born pet will not only fit right in but will thrive. If, on the other hand, you will have to leave your pet alone and confined for long periods of time, your Gemini will grow restless and unhappy. This sign craves the spotlight.

Gemini Compatibilities

Gemini-born pets get along well with most other animals, although they are a bit overactive for some of the slower-natured animal signs. If the other animal is of the opposite sex, the relationship will be smoother. Gemini pets get along equally well with dogs or cats of other signs.

Gemini's most compatible lifelong mates are Leo, Libra, Sagittarius, Pisces, and Aries.

Short-term or occasional relationships for Gemini pets are possible with Gemini, Cancer, Scorpio, Capricorn, Aquarius, and Taurus.

Gemini pets and Virgo pets are dangerous when around one another.

Gemini Pets — Gemini Pets

It will take more than one person to keep track of two Gemini-born pets in the same household. They can't stay together long before one goes wandering off to see what else it can get into. Mild conflicts of temper occur frequently. Gemini pets often leave home together, but lose each other shortly afterward and rarely return together. Owners of two Geminis are always busy keeping their animals out of trouble and chasing after the little escape artists.

Gemini Pets — Cancer Pets

Cancer-born pets and Gemini-born pets tolerate each other for short periods of time only. When kept together for long periods, they will become irritated by one another. The two won't fight viciously, but there will undoubtedly be minor skirmishes. When they play together, Gemini sparks Cancer to become more active. The disposition of Cancer pets is too calm and quiet to mix with the flightiness of Geminis.

Gemini Pets — Leo Pets

This is a lively pairing. Gemini will initiate most of the action and is willing to let the King come out on top. When Leo goes on a traveling binge, Gemini will go along. They will usually return together, sometimes with additional friends. This combination does well around crowds of people. When they are left alone, Leo will help to keep Gemini at home. They often growl and hiss at each other when playing by themselves.

Gemini Pets — Virgo Pets

Gemini pets intensely like Pisces pets; however, Pisces does not enjoy the company of Gemini. Gemini's frolicking antics are too lively and too physical for Virgo. Virgo may start to play with the reckless Gemini, but the play usually ends up as minor conflict. There is much anger between these animal signs. Virgo-

Gemini dog and cat conflicts are hazardous to their health. Bringing together Virgo and Gemini pets is flirting with danger.

Gemini Pets — Libra Pets

Gemini pets sense an attentive audience when a Libra pet is around. Gemini loves to bounce around, play, and perform for Libra. This pair is at its best and most active when there are people around. When they are left alone, Libra tires of the uncontrollable Gemini and the Gemini often leaves Libra home and wanders off, which may bring on one of Libra's claustrophobic and destructive attacks. This pairing of animal signs not only will let other animals join in their adventures but also will eagerly accept most other animal additions to the household.

Gemini Pets — Scorpio Pets

The high-spirited Gemini pet and the Scorpio pet get into lots of trouble when they are together. This pairing spells mischief. Scorpio becomes frustrated when trying to catch the fleet Gemini. Scorpio pets become jealous of the attention given Gemini pets in their presence. When these two are together in a room, hold on to the lamps and vases. They are likely to knock over all but the most stable of articles as they chase each other around.

Gemini Pets — Sagittarius Pets

These two animal signs complement each other. They are always on the go together. Equally matched in stamina and endurance, they have no problem in keeping up with each other. They will play together or by themselves; they leave each other alone as much as they are together. This twosome is difficult to keep from wandering off from home. Gemini pets and Sagittarius pets do not compete for their owner's affections or even food or toys.

Gemini Pets — Capricorn Pets

The Gemini pet is too active for Capricorn's easygoing nature. They get along well for short periods of time, then Capricorn tires of Gemini's relentless disturbances. It will be difficult to control either pet when the two are together. If this pair is kept together too long, Capricorn will reject all of Gemini's advances to play. Then Gemini will become frantic and try to involve whoever else is around in its uncontrollable excitement. Gemini and Capricorn pets will play well together if their exposure to each other is not long-term.

Gemini Pets — Aquarius Pets

When Gemini and Aquarius pets get together, they are difficult to control. They bring out each other's wild side, and you never know what they will get into. They can destroy a room in a matter of minutes. They have frequent bouts of sparring and they make lots of noise. Gemini pets and Aquarius pets will not obey their owner's commands when they are together. This pair of sun signs acts like a couple of jumping beans with each other.

Gemini Pets — Pisces Pets

There is a lot of give and take between Gemini- and Pisces-born pets. Pisces is slow to join in the action with Gemini, but eventually does. Pisces has a soothing and calming effect on Gemini. Gemini pets will even lie still long enough for Pisces pets to show them affection. Pisces and Gemini will lick, nibble, and roll around with each other in moments uncharacteristically tender for Gemini.

Gemini Pets — Aries Pets

This pairing is very lively and entertaining to be around. The nervous energy of Gemini, combined with the impulsiveness and rambunctiousness of Aries, makes for few quiet moments between the two. Gemini knows when to excite Aries to full-tilt, all-out action and when to play gently. Aries pets are attracted to Gemini pets. Their owners may think that their Aries has taken off to engage in battle with an enemy, but if a Gemini is at the end of the Aries charge, nothing more than vigorous play will result. These two signs will tire each other out, although Gemini usually outlasts Aries. Aries and Gemini get into a lot of mischief-making predicaments with each other.

Gemini Pets — Taurus Pets

Gemini pets are just too fast and excitable for the slow Taurus pet to appreciate. Taurus will not join in such frantic behavior. There is little fighting between tranquil Taurus and flighty Gemini, but there is competition for food, bones, toys, and their owner's affection. Gemini pets constantly attempt to play with Taurus pets, but their invitation is rebuffed more times than not.

The Sensitive Type:

The
CANCER
Pet

June 22 — July 22

The Cancer Personality

Cancer-born pets have the moon as their planetary ruler — very appropriate, since their moods change with the moon, causing them to be noticeably temperamental. Not prima donnas, you understand — they're too cautious and mild-mannered for outrageous drama — but they do sense alternatives in emotional temperature with unerring swiftness, and react accordingly.

Cancer-born pets are so sensitive to their surroundings, in fact, that their emotional state will almost always reflect the emotional atmosphere of the home. Their ability to mirror an owner's feelings is remarkable indeed: if you are happy, they are happy; if you get upset, they get upset. And when Cancer pets are disturbed by upheavals of any kind, they disappear silently to their favorite retreat and may well stay there for hours, even days. When in this gloomy state, the Cancer pet is unresponsive to even a much-loved owner's entreaties. Always, they will have to sense happiness or at least cheerfulness in the air before reappearing. Love wins over hunger every time.

Usually, Cancer pets are calm, quiet, docile homebodies. They are quick to anger, but they don't fight viciously or become mean. A mild growl is the usual extent of their fury.

Cancer-born pets are afraid of any animal, human or otherwise, that is bigger than they. Cancers are not fighters, and will avoid any confrontation that makes them feel uneasy. They instinctively detect aggressive opponents, too. Even male cats, known regardless of zodiacal affiliation for territorial battles, will get fewer scratches and abscesses when Cancer is their sun sign.

Are Cancers unsociable? Yes and no. Certainly Cancer-born pets are cautious when meeting your friends. They need to see a genuinely inviting response before they approach anyone. They go by their first impression and stick to it. If your Cancer pet hasn't taken to a guest on a first visit to your home, odds are it never will. For this reason, your Cancer may be disliked by some, admired by others — especially those who know just where to scratch an ear or tickle a chin. Cancers are quite affectionate to people in whom they've developed trust and will gladly take all the fondling and petting such accepted friends can dish out.

Cancer pets fear not only strangers but also loud noises. Fireworks on the Fourth of July, sonic booms, rainstorms, and loud arguments can all send the Cancer pet scurrying under the bed, where it will tremble and cry like a mouse in a lion's cage. (A high percentage of the tranquilizers that I dispense on July third are used for Cancer-born animals on July Fourth.)

Cancer-born pets are the most persistent, most accurate enemies in the zodiac. They never, ever forget unkind acts. Cancer's grudges are famous. Though usually responsive to acts of kindness, a Cancer pet will never make friends with a previous adversary, even if tempted with favorite treats or food.

Cancer pets do not like to share their home with other animals. They need to feel that their home environments are secure and stable, and any change will be met with a negative response. They especially resent sharing food, treats, or toys, and will not willingly relinquish any of their possessions, no matter how insignificant. Try to persuade them otherwise, and you may see your Cancer-born pet become violent, although the most characteristic Cancer response is to go away and sulk.

What else is on the list of Cancer peeves? Well, Cancer pets dislike traveling, too. They don't particularly care for car rides or extended walks. They are always eager and happy to return, preferring to live a secluded life among the known comforts of home. Cancer pets are not attracted to or inquisitive about humans or other animals, unless the other animal is a baby, in which case Cancers are both fascinated and patient. Wandering or roaming behavior is uncharacteristic. Many Cancer pets will remain in the front or back yards even without a fence, and really prefer to spend most of their time indoors.

Cancer-born animals love water. Cancer dogs are avid swimmers and make fine water retrievers. Even cats born under the sign of Cancer do not object to hopping in the tub once in a while.

Cancer-born pets are secretive, too, and are especially notorious for hiding food around the house. Under the cushions of the sofa, beneath newspapers, and under rugs are favorite places for them to build their delicatessens. Their bowls may be chock-full of favorite foods, but the security-obsessed Cancer pet still feels the urge to stock up. They must have their own food in their own hiding places, available whenever they want.

Not surprisingly, Cancer-born pets have a tendency to overeat, and often become far plumper than any veterinarian would advise. As the owner, you must take care not to overfeed your little Cancer gourmet.

Cancers, as noted above, have a genuine fondness for baby animals. They will very often adopt abandoned strays. Cancer dogs may even adopt a kitten. It is not unusual for female Cancers to start developing milk for the suckling orphan. Needless to say, Cancer pets get along well with children.

Many Cancers, like Scorpios, are unwanted or orphaned animals. Territory and security mean a lot to this sun sign. As long as you provide a warm and secure home, regular feedings, and affection, Cancers taken in as strays or adopted from a shelter will quickly develop strong love and attachment for their new home.

Cancer pets have extremely strong front paws and jaws. When they sink their teeth or claws into something, they hold on for dear life. You can drag them across the room with the object, or lift them off the floor with it, and they will still maintain their forceful grip. They won't let go until they are good and ready.

Cancer pets have an acute sense of touch. They will stick their unusually delicate, sensitive paws out and test a surface before moving onto it. They need to sense stability before making a move. They rarely knock things over with their paws, and have excellent coordination.

They're so balance-conscious, in fact, that some observers like to say that Cancer pets have stalky, sneaky movements. It's often hard to tell just where they are headed: their paths tend to wind and retrace and deviate to all sides, even on a simple trip across the room from Point A to Point B. Although Cancer pets are physically quieter than others, they do make soft whining and crying noises when they are upset or when things don't go their way.

Cancer pets hate major changes and react badly to them. If you move your family to a new home, your Cancer pets will take months to regain their old personalities. They prefer a secluded life of routine rather than excitement and variety, and when denied a sheltered existence very often withdraw, retreat, or otherwise deny that upsetting events are going on all around them. Cancer cats in this state find some consolation in hiding under blankets or bedspreads; Cancer dogs often spend much time in closets or out-of-the-way corners. Don't try to change their minds, just be patient.

Physically, Cancer-born pets are usually of medium height, with short legs. Their heads are often disproportionately large for their bodies. Their skeletal system consists of fine to medium bones, covered with plump musculature. They have small, even, healthy teeth. Their fur is usually a shade of brown and feels smooth and silky. If there are patches of color on the animal, one patch may be shaped like the crescent moon. Metallic colors best complement Cancers.

The Cancer Parent

Cancer-born pets are always concerned parents. They will nurture babies of any kind and are therefore well suited for rearing young. They have deep-seated maternal instincts and will shield and protect their young even into adulthood. Cancer parents will isolate themselves and their litter from outsiders, even other animals, and will devote all their time and energies to protecting the brood. They usually have large litters and are very patient with each youngster's demands. A helping hand on the owner's part is rarely needed with the Cancer pet's newborn family.

The Young Cancer

Young Cancer pets have some of the funniest faces of all animals. You can tell their states of mind by observing their expressions. They frown when they are depressed, smile when they are happy, and do everything in between as well. Cancers are usually attentive listeners and easy to manage and train, once they trust you. Do not beat them when they are young or they may retreat into gloom and never come out. They are very sensitive to reprimands, so scold them only when absolutely necessary. The young Cancer pet hates to be ignored and will cry and whine when feeling unwanted. Be sure to pick them up and give them lots of physical affection. This will build their trust in you and make them feel secure. Be consistent in your training as Cancer pets develop routines very early that will remain with them throughout their lives.

It is not easy to trick Cancer-born pets. They won't, for example, chase a ball you pretend to throw but keep in your hand.

The Healthy Cancer

Cancer pets are very susceptible to respiratory and digestive problems. Chronic bronchitis is common. Its major symptom, a persistent dry, hacking cough, will become serious if untreated. Hernias of the diaphragm and tumors of the lungs are also common in Cancer pets, as are kidney and bladder infections.

Cancer animals have unusually sensitive skin, and are vulnerable to bruises and cuts, especially about the head and face.

Vomiting is another common problem with Cancer-born pets. This may be due to diaphragm problems and simple gastritis, but Cancer pets also have a high incidence of pancreas problems, a condition that can cause persistent, sometimes violent, vomiting. Watch out for those delicate Cancer joints, too, especially the knees, where dislocating kneecaps, arthritis, and torn ligaments are often a problem.

Cancer Summary

If your household is busy and hectic, the Cancer-born pet will have trouble adapting. An Aries or Gemini would be better suited for you. Cancer pets do better in calm, quiet surroundings. They are very gentle and will make fine companions for children, even infants. They need lots of physical affection and respond to kindness. They don't do well at all when kept outdoors. They need a warm and secure home.

Cancer Pet Compatibilities

Cancer-born pets always get along better with animals smaller than themselves. They prefer to stay indoors and will usually dominate the home environment over animals of differing sun signs.

Cancer pets will readily share their homes with other Cancer, Leo, Virgo, and Pisces pets.

Although not ideally suited to sharing permanent companionship, Scorpio, Capricorn, Aquarius, Aries, Taurus, and Gemini pets make good playmates for Cancer pets.

Libras and Sagittarians do not get along well with Cancer pets.

Cancer Pets — Cancer Pets

Cancer-born pets do not feel their home is threatened when they have to share it with another Cancer. A pair of Cancer-born pets will live in their own little world. They will take care of each other and are difficult to separate. They become less responsive to what is going on around them, as they are thoroughly taken with one another. Two Cancers will fight occasionally, but the fracas will be minor. There is not much activity from two Cancer pets in the same home, as they are reluctant to move from their lounging positions.

Cancer Pets — Leo Pets

This is a very good pairing of sun signs in that both Leo's and Cancer's true personality is inspired by the other's actions. Cancer pets will get themselves into many predicaments which allow the protective Leo to come to the rescue. Cancer is content to let Leo be dominant, but Leo allows Cancer to act almost motherly towards it, taking all sorts of licks and nibbles. Leo pets make Cancer-born pets more perky.

Cancer Pets — Virgo Pets

Virgo pets and Cancer pets rarely fight, even over food. Both prefer to stay home and receive the affection of their owners. Care must be taken by the owner not to show more affection to one than to the other, since Cancer and Virgo in the same household will compete for their owner's affection. Ignoring one and favoring the other will result in one neurotic and one satisfied pet. Virgo and Cancer get along well in each other's company, and are safe to leave home alone. Be prepared to dish out lots of love and affection.

Cancer Pets — Libra Pets

Cancers are unresponsive to Libra's sincere attempts at making friends. Libras will usually withdraw and hide from Cancers. The only way these two animal signs get along is if Libras take on the characteristics of their Cancer coinhabitants. Libra will be a bit neurotic and unstable if you let this occur. There are frequent fights between Libra pets and Cancer pets, especially at first meetings.

Cancer Pets — Scorpio Pets

Scorpio-born pets are too aggressive and physical for the intuitive and docile Cancer pet. A normally quiet Cancer will even fight when a Scorpio intrudes into its home. Cancer loses the battle, and is dominated and abused by Scorpio for the remainder of their liaison. Neither Scorpio nor Cancer pets readily accept other pets into their secured territory. There is much jealousy between them when they are together.

Cancer Pets — Sagittarius Pets

These two sun signs do best if they never meet. The Cancer-born pet prefers to stay home and the Sagittarius pet prefers to leave. Sagittarius will always be running away from home if there is a Cancer occupying it. If they are locked in the same home together, Sagittarius will be anything but affectionate to Cancer. There will be much fighting, more vocal than physical. Growling, snarling, and hissing abounds in homes unfortunate enough to have a Sagittarius-Cancer pet combination.

Cancer Pets — Capricorn Pets

Cancer-born pets are attracted to Capricorn pets. They don't seem to be able to leave irresistible Capricorns alone. They do best together when they meet only occasionally, however, since their affection towards each other lasts for only short periods of time. If they are housed together briefly, the Cancer pet will not take its eyes off the Capricorn pet. If asked to share their home with Capricorn, Cancer won't let Capricorn have any peace or quiet. Every move Capricorn makes is watched and usually opposed by Cancer. The two should not be kept in the same household.

Cancer Pets — Aquarius Pets

Cancer tempers flare when their secure home environment is invaded by inquisitive Aquarians. Cancers are constantly scurrying about the house attempting to head Aquarius off at the pass. There are very few tender moments between these two animal signs. Cancers refuse to join in with Aquarians' active and impulsive behavior, and Aquarius pets refuse to be affectionate with Cancers.

Cancer Pets — Pisces Pets

This pairing of animal signs will blend harmoniously into most households. Pisces pets are gentle, even caressing, towards Cancer-born pets. Cancer will allow Pisces to be its protector, although Cancer is the boss. Both Pisces and Cancer pets will stay indoors and close to home most of the time, and violence between them will be rare. This combination of animal signs works equally well between dogs and cats.

Cancer Pets — Aries Pets

These two sun signs will not be themselves if they are together constantly in the same home. The relationship is best kept infrequent. Timid, reserved Cancer will not give in to Aries advances. Aries tries to dominate Cancer, but Cancer will never allow this to happen. Cancers become jealous when their owners show affection to Aries and they will refuse to share their food or toys or space with their rivals. Aries pets are in for a violent surprise when they invade a Cancer pet's home.

Cancer Pets — Taurus Pets

This coupling of animal sun signs will create a very quiet atmosphere. Cancer pets and Taurus pets are delicate and gentle with each other. Cancer often takes the unusual role of protector over Taurus. Both of these signs love to stay home. Cancer will stay indoors, while Taurus prefers to lounge around outdoors. Taurus and Cancer pets will eat you out of house and home if you let them. They won't leave any food lying around for one another, and will tend toward obesity when they live together and compete for food.

Cancer Pets — Gemini Pets

Cancer-born pets and Gemini-born pets tolerate each other for only short periods of time. When they are kept together for long periods, they will become irritated by one another. The two won't fight viciously, but there will undoubtedly be minor skirmishes. When they do play together, Gemini sparks Cancer to become more active. The disposition of Cancer is too calm and quiet to mix with the flightiness of Gemini.

6

Incredible Journeys:

The
LEO
Pet

July 23 — August 22

The Leo Personality

King Leo likes to be dominant in the animal kingdom. Canine or feline, your Leo will strut around with the grace and dignity of royalty.

Leo purebreds walk tall with their heads held high, certain they are the result of generations of selected breeding. Leo not-so-purebreds move the same way, seemingly basking in the knowledge that they are superior to the rest of the animal kingdom.

Ruled by the sun and fire signs, Leo pets have an insatiable desire to explore the unknown. Their curious natures will often lead them into potentially explosive situations. Your Leo cat may venture into another feline's turf. Your Leo dog may confront the local population of wandering canine minstrels. There is rarely a need to worry, for the King is a born leader, easily recognized by his compatriots. Leo will not join the new gang until he has assessed all the potential hostilities and is confident that in a short time he will be the leader.

Leo is second only to its zodiac counterpart, Sagittarius, in needing room to roam. The incidence of roaming may be decreased by satisfying its curiosity. Take your pet on as many different trips as you can. Make each trip an adventure — a visit to the park or woods for Leo dogs, access in the house to off-limits areas for the Leo cat. Let Leo explore and investigate. The result will be a much more contented monarch.

Whether it's Top Cat sitting on his trash can throne in the alley, or the leader of the hounds at the fox hunt, chances are he's a Leo. Strong of body and will, Leo's personality will project him to the top of his class. Leo pets make excellent show animals.

The leadership qualities of your Leo pet will invariably cause him to gather a menagerie of cohorts. Don't fear, your house will not become a zoo. Leo will rarely let a common companion into his castle. The visitors, however, should be treated with the respect due members of the Royal Family, for, once established, Leo's animal and human friendships and allegiances are lifelong. Leo will always be loyal and trustworthy if you give them freedom, confidence, and affectionate support.

Since Leo's castle is your home, a Leo dog makes an excellent protector, and even Leo cats make phenomenal guards against smaller unwanted intruders. But remember, Leos become frustrated and humiliated when forced into submission and must be allowed their freedom, especially indoors. An extra chair in the living room is a fitting throne for this loyal friend.

A note of caution. Do not give in to *every* demand the King makes, or your pet may soon rule you. Mild vocal discipline, from the time you meet your Leo, will usually suffice to promote a harmonious environment.

Thinking about acquiring a mature Leo? If a Leo has been treated properly, that is, if it feels its kingly stature, it may become seriously depressed in a new setting. Leo hates being dethroned. Acceptance of the new domain will take months or even years. If the previous owners visit the new home after Leo has settled in they will be scorned, ignored, and embarrassed by the situation. Leo is not very forgiving, and has an astute memory. This is also why you must be careful to raise your Leo with mild discipline.

Unselfishness is another trait of Leo pets. Their dominance is not accomplished arrogantly, but rather with a willingness to please all those around. A little approval on your part for an act well done goes a long way in keeping Leos satisfied. At their best, Leos make their owners proud. Mistreated, Leos cause confusion all around.

All Leos, male and female, will develop particularly strong bonds to the children they are around. Young children are innocent and honest, traits to which Leos respond. They therefore make good pets for families.

Leos rise to the occasion during emergencies. Their loyalty and devotion to friends enable them to throw caution to the wind when necessary. When Leo's courage erupts, there is no room left for fear. Leo pets are often the ones you hear about sacrificing themselves to protect or save loved ones.

In appearance, Leo-born pets share distinguishing features regardless of their breed. They have the look of nobility. Males are strong and commanding in physique with strong jaws. Eyes are of the richest brown or sky blue and have a deep, penetrating quality. Strong bony frames with firm musculature are characteristic. Their gaits are graceful, smooth, and sure, and they possess a composure reminiscent of the jungle lion.

The Leo female will be unmistakably feminine, yet strong in appearance. Males are attracted to her, and she will be friendly with all of them. She thrives on attention, from both her owner and her own kind. Among other females, she is the flirty, friendly standout. The Leo female can hold her own in activities thought to be reserved for the male of the species. She is athletic, a leader in her own right, a bit aloof, but always graceful.

Leo animals are most comfortable when surrounded by the colors of nature in autumn.

When content in their domain, Leos age gracefully. Periods of deep serene rest increase as the years go by — asleep, but glowing with remembered glory. Satisfied with all their previous conquests, old Leos respond only to new and intriguing challenges.

The Leo Parent

Leos' offspring will be showered and protected with their parental love. They have one of the strongest of nature's instincts to protect and raise their young. Leo fathers radiate pride and instill their young with poise. Leo mothers devote themselves to nurturing in a gentle and dignified manner. So strong is this maternal instinct that even when the young are mature their mother's watchful eyes are always upon them. It is best to establish a constant routine for the new Leo family. Do not stray too much from your daily schedule of feeding, time spent outdoors, play, and periods of undisturbed rest. Leos will adapt their parental functions to fit the schedule. Much can be learned about proper child rearing by observing these noble parents.

The Young Leo

The Leo pet's personality traits are strongly influenced by that of its natural parents. If you are obtaining a newborn Leo, take this into consideration. Do parents of your chosen Leo have the disposition and traits that you want in your pet? If so, leave him there until he is eight or nine weeks of age. If not, remove your impressionable Leo at six or seven weeks. He will then acquire traits influenced by those in his new surroundings.

House training or litter-box training is easily accomplished with Leos. Once they realize the boundaries of their castle, Leos will not wish to soil their own homes. Frequent trips outdoors for a puppy, and showing your kitten the litter-box at the appropriate time, usually suffice in the training department. Continue this routine until your Leo is at least six months old.

Leo puppies and kittens are very active. They will bounce their way into your heart in minutes. Keep them happy and they will always feel free. This is a must for the King of Beasts, or you will soon be taking your Leo to the pet psychiatrist. Always remember that discipline must be handled gently. Don't break your pet's spirit. Young Leos learn quickly when given only encouragement. Overlook mistakes, and reward triumphs with kindness.

Strong attachment to littermates is a trait of Leos, and separation from them causes trauma. Give your pet extra attention during this first emotional crisis, and your investment will yield lifelong returns. Maturity comes quickly for Leos, so decide early about confining during heat periods, spaying, etc.

The Healthy Leo

Big-hearted Leo sometimes has physical trouble in this area. In Leo cats, cardiomyopathy occurs. Difficulty in breathing, shortness of breath, and rapid shallow respirations are signs of this problem. Irregular and abnormal heartbeats are also found in Leo animals. As Leos age, congestive heart failure is common. Because of their susceptibility to heart ailments, be sure to have your Leo dog on heartworm preventative medicine.

Spinal problems are also prevalent in Leo. Ruptured disks, pinched nerves, curvatures of the spine, and neck injuries are commonplace. The shoulder disease, osteochondritis, appears frequently in the young. Fortunately, most of these conditions are easy to treat.

As in some ancient aristocracies, seizures occur often in Leos. When caught early, treatment is very successful. Liver problems and epilepsy usually cause the seizures.

Diseases of the upper respiratory tract, in both cats and dogs, also have an affinity for Leo, as do hepatitis and diseases of the liver veins. Seizures, weight loss, and disorientation in the immature Leo animal may indicate this set of problems.

Leo Summary

If you are looking for a pet that you and your family can dominate, that will follow every miniscule command, that will be happy in the garage or on a leash, Leo is not for you. The King will not go second class. But if you are willing to share your castle and treat Leo with dignity and respect, that royal manner will permeate your surroundings. Content Leo pets will exude nobility to the end, trustworthy and devoted to those who treat them fairly, yet the lords of their earthly domains.

Leo Pet Compatibilities

Leo-born pets are compatible with most other animal sun signs. Leo animals will protect their animal friends from dangers.

Leo pets are willing to share their domains with pets of the following signs: Leo, Libra, Sagittarius, Capricorn, Aries, Taurus, Gemini, and Cancer.

Virgo or Pisces pets are tolerated by Leo pets for only short periods of time.

Scorpios and Aquarians spell trouble when combined with Leos.

Leo Pets — Virgo Pets

Leo-born pets like to play with Virgo pets, who seem willing to let Leo lead the way as they follow. Yet Virgos get bored playing with the King for any extended length of time. When they are housed together, Virgo tires of following Leo around playing the submissive role and this takes the King down a couple of notches. Leo may become frustrated and depressed with the unresponsive Virgo around. This is not healthy for the King. Leo and Virgo pets get along best when they visit each other only occasionally.

Leo Pets — Libra Pets

This is a very active combination of animal sun signs, one that brings out the best in both. Libra will have a settling effect on Leo and Leo's wandering will be decreased significantly. Libra tames the overaggressiveness sometimes found in Leo pets. Leo's enthusiasm for exploring and playing with children will stimulate Libra to join in. These two animal signs are very responsive to each other's actions. They make good companions for the family and for each other.

Leo Pets — Scorpio Pets

Fierce battles and utter chaos result when these two animal sun signs are brought together. There is a constant struggle for the dominant position. Leo pets become very vocal and will bark, howl, or meow ferociously when Scorpio pets are around. Neither Leo nor Scorpio will completely give in to the other. It is best to keep these animals in separate rooms if for some reason they have to be in the same home.

Leo Pets — Leo Pets

This pairing works especially well if the two Leos are of different sexes or different species. Neither will give in to the other, refusing to have their noble noses rubbed in the dirt. They play roughly, tumbling over and around each other, and dragging each other by the scruff of the neck. There will, however, be lots of quiet and gentle moments, usually outside while they are relaxing under a shade tree. When two Leos are together, they draw the attention of most passersby.

Leo Pets — Sagittarius Pets

Animals of these two signs have lots of fun together. Sagittarians will be the more active, causing Leo pets to quicken their usually strolling pace. This twosome often becomes active during the night. When they are out on the go, Leo will let Sagittarius do the initial exploring and take all the chances, standing by as the lookout and warning or protecting Sagittarius from danger.

Leo Pets — Capricorn Pets

This is a good combination of animal signs. Leo and Capricorn can be themselves with each other. Capricorn will be excited by Leo's carefree and assertive nature, and Leo will feel like the King though the kingdom will be limited by Capricorn. Capricorn will live peacefully in a space separate from the King's. With Leo around, Capricorn becomes more outgoing and more vocal. They take on a carefree and happy disposition in one another's presence. A Leo cat and a Capricorn dog make a constantly entertaining pair in the home.

Leo Pets — Aquarius Pets

Owners should keep Leo and Aquarius pets separate. Their tempers are short with each other and fierce battles erupt when they are brought together. Human intervention may be needed to prevent serious injury. When they first meet, animals of these two sun signs seem friendly and fascinated with each other, but sniffing soon turns into biting.

Leo Pets — Pisces Pets

Leo pets make Pisces pets less inhibited and the two will play actively together. Leo will guard Pisces like a favorite toy. Pisces will be submissive while Leo dominates the relationship. The constant prodding of Pisces by Leo often leads to a rare outburst of temper from Pisces pets. If these two are kept together for extended periods of time, Pisces has a tranquilizing effect on Leo.

Leo Pets — Aries Pets

Another exciting combination of animal signs is Aries and Leo, especially when Leo is of the feline species and Aries is of the canine species. The two will get along very well in the same home, each respecting the other's territory and possessions. This is a fun-loving pair and fighting is rare. Aries pets are good for Leo pets in that they liven up depressed Leos and quiet Leo desires to be dominant.

Leo Pets — Taurus Pets

There is lots of noise when Taurus and Leo pets are together. The barking, snarling, and meowing does not usually lead to fighting; these two signs just make each other very vocal. Leo is usually dominant with Taurus following along. Leo pets make Taurus pets become more active. Taurus will give Leo the run of the house.

Leo Pets — Gemini Pets

This is a lively pairing. Gemini will initiate most of the action and is willing to let the King come out on top. When Leo goes on a traveling binge, Gemini will stay right by Leo's side. They will usually return together, if not with additional friends. This combination does well around crowds of people. When they are left alone Leo will help to keep Gemini at home. They often growl and hiss at each other when playing by themselves.

Leo Pets — Cancer Pets

This is a very good pairing in that both Leo's and Cancer's true personalities are brought forth by the other's actions. Cancer pets will get themselves into many predicaments that will allow the protective Leo pet to come to the rescue. Cancer is content to let Leo be dominant. Leo pets allow Cancer pets to act almost motherly towards them, taking all the licks and nibbles Cancer will give. Leo will make Cancer perkier.

7

A World of Their Own:

The
VIRGO
Pet

August 23 — September 22

The Virgo Personality

Virgo pets tend to be timid, shy, and uneasy around strangers or new situations. Virgos are ruled by the planet Mercury. They will avoid any newcomers into their territory. They are more at ease by themselves, perhaps playing gently with a butterfly or baby bird.

Virgos are intrigued by living creatures smaller than themselves. I knew a Virgo English setter that became fascinated with worms, and would stay outdoors for hours in the rain to play with the wiggly creatures. This is just one example of how Virgos withdraw into their own worlds of minutiae. Virgos are able to find pleasure in things around them which are overlooked by the majority of their kind.

Virgo is slow to make new acquaintances. If you wish your Virgo pet to be friends with the neighbor's pet, introduce them while your Virgo is young. Even then it will take many contacts before a friendship grows. Virgos are very careful in associations with other animals or humans. However, they are dependable, gentle, and sympathetic with known family members.

If ever an animal is known to show sympathy, it is a Virgo. Virgo knows instinctively when those around are anything less than healthy. When you are depressed and lonely, Virgo companions will come to you affectionately. When you hurt yourself, they will scamper around as though they feel the pain. Virgo knows how to comfort.

Virgo animals love to be trained. They sense a need to perfect their owners' requests. Virgos make the finest working dogs. They are also excellent at providing dependable service to the handicapped. Retrieving, hunting, pointing, and learning tricks are also strong areas. They may not be naturals at what they are asked to do, but with lots of eager practice they will learn the task. Virgo will be extremely hard-working and generous in return for a little physical affection and a clean environment. Your Virgo pet will be satisfied just to serve you.

The Virgo pet is not often outwardly affectionate to its owner. Springing up or pouncing when you come home is not in their makeup. Neither is slurping your face. They are loving in a much more reserved way. Lying in the evening with head gently perched on your warm foot is more their style, or perhaps sitting pressed against your leg when you are talking to neighbors. They usually have restrained emotions. Your Virgo pets will be content to share an evening with you in front of the fireplace.

Although Virgos do not show extreme amounts of outward affection, they yearn so for you to show affection toward *them*. Virgos need to be touched frequently and kindly to remain stable. When warm feelings are not demonstrated, Virgos come apart emotionally. They may become very withdrawn, even to the point of retreating to their favorite hiding place for hours or exhibiting uncharacteristic outbursts of temper. After a time, however, they regain their composure and return to normal.

It is hard to keep a Virgo animal's attention for very long. Remember this when trying to train your little Virgo, for this trait is magnified in the young. Restlessness throughout their juvenile months is normal. They just can't sit still.

Virgo pets are usually major procrastinators. The Virgo cat will study the situation extensively before making a leap from the chair to your best lampshade. The Virgo dog will cross a stream by placing one foot at a time in the water, then withdraw and start over again and again. Be patient, for Virgos are just taking in everything around them before choosing a suitable course. Once Virgos have mastered a feat, they will repeat it precisely and accurately every time.

You may have a hard time getting your Virgo pet to eat the food you select.

Many Virgos are more finicky than Morris the Cat. It is best to stick to a brand of food your Virgo likes, unless it is not balanced, rather than try to force a change for economics or convenience.

Bathe your Virgo pet very rarely, for this is one of the cleanest animals you will come across. Your feline Virgo will so meticulously groom every strand of fur that you will probably have to administer medication to prevent fur-balls and gagging. Virgo the dog will likewise attempt all the hygienic antics of a raccoon to keep clean. Certain situations are sure to require bathing Virgo, but you will never clean the store out of pet shampoo.

Is your Virgo-born kitty avoiding its litterbox? Does it prefer the soil in your plant pots, or use an unoccupied room in the house? Sticklers for hygienic conditions, Virgo felines may refuse to use their litterbox unless it is freshened after each visit.

You will cause less anxiety in your Virgo dog if you keep its bathroom area clean also. They will sneer in disgust when forced to tiptoe to avoid previous droppings. Your Virgo pet will make you feel ashamed if its meticulously kept body is sullied.

The physical characteristics of Virgos are usually deceiving. They tend to be a little on the small side, although well proportioned. Their bones are fine to medium-sized. Very lean but well-defined musculature covers their skeleton. Glossy, well-groomed fur makes them gleam. Green eyes are common among Virgos. They are attractive in appearance, and seemingly fragile, like a fine work of porcelain. Virgo's movements are always graceful, like those of a ballet dancer.

As delicate as Virgos may appear, handling with kid gloves is not necessary. They are stronger and have more stamina than many of the more massive of their species. Pound for pound, Virgo may be the strongest of its kind.

Training your Virgo is an easy task. Once a feat is accomplished it will be repeated the same way every time. They love to serve their masters. Virgo receives satisfaction from working.

Remember that your Virgo's nature is not to be too outwardly affectionate. It will be up to you to initiate most of the physical contact which is essential to your Virgo's mental health.

Many owners take Virgo's precise and repetitive actions for granted. Not until a friend marvels at such perfect feats do they realize what a unique friend they have.

As adult Virgo pets age, a sense of security sets in. They become more emotionally outgoing. It's as if they are going through a second puppyhood or kittenhood. They become less inhibited.

Yellow, green, and mixtures in between are the colors best suited for your Virgo pet.

The Virgo Parent

As parents, female Virgos yearn for offspring. Their personalities will be enhanced by allowing them this satisfaction. The Virgo mother wants her nest spotless, and will welcome your help in keeping it so. You may feel free to interact with your Virgo's newborn family from day one. An overbearing attitude is rare among Virgo parents. Puppies or kittens will be allowed their freedom to develop as individuals, but their Virgo mother's watchful and protective eyes are always upon them. Small litters are common from Virgo mothers.

If your pregnant Virgo pet gives birth in a spot other than the one you have picked out, it is best to leave her in the area of her choice. For some reason your choice did not suit her needs. Have confidence that Virgo mothers know best. Work with and around her decision.

If mother Virgo has a weak youngster in the new crew, she may nurture the unfortunate one to the neglect of the others. Take the newborn to your veterinarian to be sure its situation is not hopeless. The Virgo mother may let the others deteriorate while consumed in caring for the sick one.

Male Virgo pets will delegate as much of the parental duties as they can to you and the mother of their young. If he sees they are neglected, then his presence will be known. If for some reason the young are not receiving enough attention, your male Virgo will spend more time with his babies. He prefers to take over parental responsibilities once the young are old enough to move about freely. At that point father Virgo will begin teaching his young about the vast world they have entered.

The Young Virgo

Virgo puppies and kittens are very serene. They are peaceful in their inner world. Virgo is less vocal than many others of their species when young. You may not hear a bark, yipe, or meow for weeks after taking them home.

They need to become comfortable with their new surroundings before they gain the confidence to explore and play freely. Do not expect too much of them the first few days. Little Virgo will make up for this reticence in the days that follow.

Once at ease in their new setting, Virgo will come out of its shell of shyness and form intimate bonds with those around. If there are other animals, your Virgo will start to imitate their actions. Virgo learns quickly, and playing copycat is one way they do so. The other method young Virgo pets use to educate themselves takes much longer. When confronted with a new situation, your little Virgo will stop cold in its tracks. Virgo's curiosity will not get the best of them. Careful study of the new challenge is necessary before Virgo makes a move. All the alternatives and possible consequences are taken into account. Once the decision is made, Virgo's plan is put into action. If the decision is correct and things go smoothly, your Virgo then will respond in the same way when facing the same situation. Virgo pets become creatures of habit, and unless their calculated response is disrupted, they will not change.

You will no doubt have trouble feeding your little Virgos. Find a balanced name-brand puppy or kitten diet that they like and that agrees with them and stick to it. Any abrupt dietary change may result in digestive upsets. A veterinarian-recommended vitamin-mineral supplement will help to offset the dietary problems commonly found in the finicky Virgo.

Keep little Virgos clean. If they should get something on their coat that doesn't come off easily, they will exhaust themselves trying to remove it. Virgo pets crave cleanliness. Baths at times like these, or whenever Virgos get dirty, will be appreciated. Use a cream rinse after each bath so as not to dry out the pet's sensitive skin.

The Healthy Virgo

Hypochondria is a Virgo specialty. Virgo pets, when unhappy, will display behavior that will make you think they are sick. You can't take a chance. Their health is dependent upon you. So take them to the vet, but don't be surprised when the alarms are false.

Parasites are another Virgo problem. Worms are common in all animals, but especially in Virgos. Have them checked regularly, particularly when they are young. Heartworm prevention is a must for the parasite-sensitive Virgo.

Digestive systems are a Virgo weak point. Look especially for:

- Dilation of the stomach in large size Virgo dogs.

- Diarrheas from problems of the small and large intestines (enteritis and colitis).

- Malabsorption and improper digestion of food due to pancreas problems.

- Vomiting from stomach or pancreas ailments.

- Too small an opening out of the stomach.

- Cancer of the intestinal tract.

- Consuming foreign bodies.

- Intestinal twists and obstructions.

Many Virgos are subject to reproductive system problems:

- ovary problems in females, testicle problems in males. (Tumors, cysts, and abnormalities are all part of this large clinical picture.)

• Infected uterus, in female Virgos, is often seen as well.

Knees are Virgo territory, too, whether osteochondritis of the knee cartilage, or accidents to the knee area causing fractures and torn ligaments. (This may be a lifelong troublesome injury for Virgo.)

Many Virgos are especially susceptible to various chronic, debilitating diseases. The most common are:

• Leukemia (in Virgo felines especially)

• Infectious peritonitis (in Virgo cats)

• Cancer

• Anemia

• Chronic kidney disease.

Virgo Summary

The Virgo pet is perfect for owners who love to shower their charges with affection, for Virgos will respond in kind. They will be exceedingly sympathetic and comforting, and are easy to train. Their dependability and empathetic quality make Virgos prized pets.

Virgo Pet Compatibilities

Virgo pets are for the most part shy around other animals when they first meet. Don't judge the relationship by this first encounter. After more exposure to other animals, Virgo's friendship bonds will take hold.

If the other animal is smaller than your Virgo pet, problems with the companionship will be few and far between. If the other animal is larger, much more time will be needed for their relationship to form.

The best sun signs for Virgo-born pets to share a home with are: Virgo, Capricorn, Pisces, Taurus, and Cancer.

Animals born under the signs of Aries, Leo, Libra, Sagittarius, and Scorpio make better casual acquaintances than housemates for Virgo pets.

Animals with Gemini or Aquarius as their sun sign should be watched carefully when confronting your Virgo pet.

Virgo Pets — Virgo Pets

This will be a harmonious relationship in your household. Even Virgo dogs and Virgo cats get along well. Their similar gentle natures and habits make for a good match. They love to do things together, sharing their experiences. They do well when left alone together and will not need your constant involvement in their interactions. A Virgo pet will scamper to the rescue if the other yips or meows from pain or fear. Your home will be relatively calm with two Virgo pets.

Virgo Pets — Libra Pets

Libra-born pets are usually unresponsive to Virgo pets. Librans do not usually fight with Virgos; they ignore them. Libra does not take to the shyness and tenderness exhibited by Virgo. They prefer more active interactions, such as with family members. Virgo pets will often get the blame for deeds that were done by a Libra housemate. When you arrive home to find the plants knocked over and the carpet chewed up, chances are that Libra and not Virgo was the culprit. Virgos have a hard time expressing their personalities when Libras are constantly overshadowing them.

Virgo Pets — Scorpio Pets

Unless they are forced to live together, Virgo pets and Scorpio pets get along well. They let each other be themselves. The good points of both come out when they are casual acquaintances. Scorpio will be lively, entertaining, and physical. Virgo will be compassionate, tender, and shy. They will not compete for the affection of people around them. When kept together for extended lengths of time, Scorpios will become aggressive toward Virgos. Dogs and cats of differing Scorpio and Virgo signs are usually enemies at all times.

Virgo Pets — Sagittarius Pets

Virgo pets and Sagittarius pets, dogs and cats alike, have fun playing together. Often Sagittarius will not finish the game or activity they have started together, leaving a bewildered Virgo. They don't do well when they are constantly together in the same home, as Sagittarius is always abandoning the Virgo pet in the midst of Virgo's happiness and excitement. This makes Virgo reluctant to show affection toward Sagittarius and other household inhabitants. When the relationship is more casual, Virgo will romp and play with Sagittarius as if they were still small. Keep a close eye on your Virgo pet when you let it out to play with the neighbor's Sagittarius pet, as Virgo is very likely to follow wandering Sagittarius on an extended excursion.

Virgo Pets — Capricorn Pets

Virgo pets and Capricorn pets complement each other in a household. There will not be much barking or meowing in your home with these two. They will play together for hours. They are very affectionate towards each other, and will lie around in the evenings licking and cleaning one another's fur. Virgo pets and Capricorn pets make a good combination for breeding. This builds the affectionate bond between them and they will be content to stay home. Fighting between these two pet signs is rare, even between cats and dogs.

Virgo Pets — Aquarius Pets

The more distance the better between these two pet signs. The problem is not fighting, but the expression of bad traits brought about by their meeting. Aquarius pets get along with most other animals, but Virgo pets bring out their worst. Aquarians will bark or meow endlessly in the presence of Virgos. They will become unresponsive to their owner's requests, and even unmanageable. Virgo pets become withdrawn when they are around Aquarius pets, retreating into their shell of shyness and sometimes staying there for days. A backyard fence will provide Virgo with the territorial security needed from their strange Aquarian neighbor. They will have their normal personality as long as there is no direct contact with Aquarius.

Virgo Pets — Pisces Pets

Virgo pets and Pisces pets form a happy and docile union. They are both a bit shy, and are compassionate to their owners and to each other. Virgo usually dominates this relationship, although not to the point of inhibiting Pisces' personality. Pisces will bring Virgo out of its shyness and they will play together frequently. The playfulness will start gently and will culminate with playful growling, snarling, and thrashing around. This is usually uncharacteristic of both of these animal signs. They are happy and genuinely relaxed with each other's company. Although the Virgo pet is usually the dominant one, it will acquire some of the Pisces pet's traits. Virgo pets will become more outwardly affectionate to humans when under the influence of a Pisces pet.

Virgo Pets — Aries Pets

Aries-born pets are too aggressive for the timid Virgo pet. The high-strung nature of Aries means it can totally dominate Virgo. Aries is attracted to Virgo and will enthusiastically go out of its way to aggressively greet the withdrawn Virgo. The Virgo pet will try to accommodate Aries. Virgo pets do not have the stamina of Aries pets and Aries will eventually boss Virgo around. Meetings between Virgo and Aries pets should therefore be kept short. Constant companionship between the two will lead to a onesided, Aries-dominated relationship.

Virgo Pets — Taurus Pets

Taurus-born pets love all Virgo-born animals. The bond and friendship between these two pet signs is likely to be lifelong. They are comfortable and content in each other's company. Even a large Taurus dog will play tenderly with a Virgo kitten. Both Virgo and Taurus are cautious when meeting strangers, so they take comfort and security in each other. Taurus pets will not take advantage of the easily dominated Virgo pet. Both Tauruses and Virgos are content to stay home in each other's company, yet their personalities remain separate and distinct.

Virgo Pets — Gemini Pets

The frolicking antics of Gemini pets are too lively and too physical for Virgo pets. Virgo may start to play with reckless Gemini, but it usually ends up in a minor conflict of tempers. There is much anger between these animal signs. Virgo-Gemini dog and cat conflicts are hazardous to their health. Bringing together Virgo and Gemini pets is flirting with danger.

Virgo Pets — Cancer Pets

Virgo pets and Cancer pets rarely fight, even over food. They prefer to stay home and receive the affection of their owners. The owner must take care not to show more affection to one than to the other. Cancer and Virgo pets in the same household will compete for their owner's affection. Ignoring one and favoring the other will result in one neurotic and one satisfied pet. Virgo pets and Cancer pets get along well and are safe to leave home alone. Be prepared to dish out lots of love and affection.

Virgo Pets — Leo Pets

Virgo-born pets like to play with Leo pets. They seem willing to let Leo lead the way as they follow along. Virgo pets get bored playing with the King for any extended length of time. When they are housed together, Virgo tires of playing the submissive role, and this takes the King down a couple of notches. Leo may become frustrated and depressed with the unresponsive Virgo around. This is not healthy for the King. Leo and Virgo pets get along best when they visit each other only occasionally.

8

Equal Affection:

The
LIBRA
Pet

September 23 — October 23

The Libra Personality

Libra-born pets make harmonious additions to any household. They are rarely troublesome and will blend with either small or large families, fitting right in to family routines so well it will seem as if they were always there. Everyone in the family will have a devoted companion, because each family member will feel that Libra likes them best. Libras aren't hypocritical or fawning, but they do have a way of getting on everyone's good side, and invariably choose a lifestyle that takes the smoothest of routes.

True to its sign, the balanced scales of justice and fair dealing, your Libra pet will share time equally among family members, comfortable in any lap, happy to supervise any activity. Libra pets are rarely the topic of quarrels, largely because they avoid rocking their domestic boat.

For the most part, Libra pets are extremely mild-mannered. They love to play along, and are thus very easy to dupe or trick. Due to their inborn sweet tempers, a fierce or mean Libra pet is almost unheard of. Their appearance, too, is one of gentleness. Libra couldn't scare a flea if it tried. To make a watch dog or household protector out of a Libra pet can be difficult, even impossible. Companionship is their forte, and they know it.

Although Libras make easygoing pets, they do possess a stubborn streak that will occasionally expose itself when you least expect it, usually in the form of a snarl or howl of temper. Libras' stubbornness may also manifest itself as unresponsiveness. They will withdraw to a secluded space and not respond to your attempts at arousing or placating them. When this happens, try playing soft, classical music to them, since this has a remarkably soothing effect on Libra pets and usually puts them in a more amiable frame of mind.

Libras are very sensitive to raised voices or arguments going on around them, and will quickly remove themselves from any seemingly hostile environment. If they can't be seen, they feel safe. Libras will reappear with their usual sunny disposition intact once things have settled down. For this reason, all you need do to reprimand your Libra pet is scold it verbally.

Libras are ruled by the planet Venus, but most owners find that an intense sex drive is not part of their Libra pet's personality. This is fortunate, for all of the bad habits that accompany this drive will not develop in your little Libran family member.

Male Libra dogs, for instance, typically are not roamers. Libra tomcats may go traveling, but only for leisurely strolls, which rarely involve territorial fights.

Female Libra dogs may attract males when they are in heat, but they don't go out looking. Female Libra felines, too, tend to be less restless and less vocal than others when in heat.

Libra pets do not enjoy being left alone, and are most prone, of all the animal sun signs, to acute claustrophobia. The smaller the area you confine them to when left by themselves, the unhappier they become. If you lock Libra in a small room, you may find the room demolished or soiled when you return. Give them a larger area in the house for freedom when you leave. Soothing music left on the radio when you leave also helps control such behavior problems.

If you should invite a couple of friends over to your home, the Libra pet will be cheerful, unaffected, and affectionate. But if a party-size crowd should appear, don't expect to see your Libra until everything has quieted down. The increase in noise level, along with the activities of social interaction, confuse them. They are not shy or timid, just perplexed by the situation. The Libra pet cannot make sense out of crowds (too much information, too much sensory stimulation), and would rather leave than try to figure them out.

Feeding your Libra will be no problem. Just the opposite, in fact. They are not gluttons, but will eat almost anything. Combine this trait with the Libra pet's almost lazy nature, and you have the explanation for their tendency to become overweight.

Unless scavenging outdoors is the way your Libra obtains much of its daily ration, you as the owner control the situation. Be careful in the amount of food you give. Talk to the kids about giving too many treats and don't let your Libra pet stay lazy. More exercise — walks, playing with a string, throwing a ball for your Libra to retrieve — is often the answer.

Libra-born animals do not get angry easily. It will take quite a bit of teasing and prodding before their anger threshold is reached. Then they explode like a keg of dynamite. They will tolerate a lot, but hate extremes.

If for some reason Libra pets are abused, mistreated, or embarrassed, they will probably appear to take it in stride. Don't be fooled, however: delayed revenge is bound to occur. At some future time, when you least expect it, the Libra pet will get even. The revenge is not usually violent. It will most likely take the form of stubbornness, perhaps embarrassing the culprit.

Libra-born pets are difficult to train alone. "The more the better" seems to be their philosophy when it comes to performing. If other animals are around, they will eagerly join the team and flawlessly execute the requests. By themselves, they lack interest. Sharing the adventure is more their style. Be patient while training Libra. If the feat is only half mastered, chances are they understand what you want them to do. They have learned it, but they won't always do it.

Libra pets love having a backyard or field they can visit. They make better indoor pets when they realize this is available for their explorations. Apartments do not suit them very well. If your Libra lives in an apartment, pay frequent visits back to nature to enhance their personality. Libra's domesticated side must be balanced with their natural yearnings.

Libra pets enjoy mild climates. The hot or cold seasons cause them discomfort. They tend towards laziness when environmental conditions are harsh. Spring and fall weather complement Libra's health, both physically and mentally.

Libra pets show few outward signs of illness when they are sick. They look healthy until they become seriously or critically ill. Close observation of Libra is needed to assess their health. Any abnormalities in their daily functions, activity, behavior, or appearance should alert the Libra owner to a potential medical problem and should get immediate attention.

Libra pets have naturally graceful lines. Their stature does not hide excess weight. They tend to be tall compared to the rest of their breed types. Their medium-sized bone structure always appears solid. Their musculature is lean with sloping and blending lines. There is a propensity for curly, wiry, and rough coats amongst Libra pets. Long, graceful heads and necks are common. They have a meek, mild look.

White and light pastel colors complement Libra's appearance.

The Libra Parent

As parents, Libra pets will be gentle with their offspring but will keep the youngsters in line and quickly scold or reprimand undesirable behavior. Favoring one individual in the litter is uncharacteristic of Libra parents. The youngsters are treated as a unit. They will all receive the same amount of attention from the Libra mother or father. Mother Libra will see that all the young are fed their fair share so the stronger cannot take advantage of the weaker. Uniform, healthy, and large litters are the result.

You will marvel at mother or father Libra's ability to keep the herd of little ones together and in order on their early family outings. Libra parents are able to keep control until their young reach five or six weeks of age. Then your work will begin.

The Young Libra

Young Libra puppies or kittens are real charmers. Their mild manners and gentle expressions make them appear totally helpless. Young Libras have a very strong attachment to one another and will share everything. When young Libra puppies or kittens find something of interest, they will take it back to the others. There will then be a cooperative effort to decide the fate of the new-found commodity.

When food is put before the ravenous Libra crew, no fighting occurs. All is willingly shared.

Little Libras will always cry when removed from their siblings. Likewise, they will be ecstatic when put back into their family sanctuary. It is often hard for a prospective owner to pick just one Libra youngster. You may find yourself coming home with two or more. You may tell yourself you will find homes for the rest, but unless you are prepared to keep them all, be sure and choose just one. Sibling bonds become stronger as your little Libras age and it becomes harder to separate them. Check with friends who have brother and sister pets. Chances are they have a couple of Libras.

Libra youngsters are not very aggressive. Their nature leans more towards pacifism. They enjoy being exposed to nature, if the weather is agreeable. Going on long, leisurely walks is Libra's idea of a good time.

Young Libra ears are sensitive to loud noises. Scolding them for bad behavior is as effective as spanking them. They enjoy the company of humans.

The Healthy Libra

Libra pets are among the healthiest you can own. They hide any illnesses well — so well, in fact, that when they seem at all under the weather, you can be sure they're considerably sicker than they appear. Libras are especially vulnerable to kidney and bladder problems. Hydrouretheu, or dilated uretes, is indicated by the constant dripping of urine, and is seen frequently in spayed Libra female dogs. Kidney infections can cause your Libra to walk around with a painfully hunched back. Other Libras are vulnerable to chronic hepatitis, whose symptoms include loss of appetite, vomiting, increase in water consumption, and irritation accompanied by weight loss.

Cystitis, or an infection in the urinary bladder, is especially common in Libra pets, and is often first noticed via blood in the urine or increased frequency of urinations. Calculi, or stools in the bladder, are another common Libra problem, as is (especially in male Libra cats) urethal obstruction.

Libras are also vulnerable to blood difficulties — heartworms, or parasites in the blood, and anemia being the most frequently seen — and to skeletal-system problems, especially ruptured disks and calcification of the spinal cord, which in the older Libra can lead to paralysis of the rear legs.

Libra Summary

A Libra pet makes an excellent addition to any family. They are not soloists. Family interaction is essential for their best personality development and for sustaining their innately gentle, cooperative nature.

Libra Pet Compatibilities

The mild-mannered Libra-born pet rarely causes much commotion or conflict in a household with other animals. But don't mistake acquiescence for indifference in your Libra. They've got plenty of opinions on preferred company, but are often just too polite (or too lazy) to make such preferences clear. Changes in Libra pets' personalities when influenced by animals of different sun signs are subtle but definite.

Libra pets are most compatible with other Libras, Sagittarius, Aquarius, Taurus, Gemini, and Leo.

Other pets with signs of Capricorn, Pisces, Aries, and Virgo get along best with Libra pets when their meetings are occasional.

Cancer and Scorpio pets do not make good companions for Libra pets.

Libra Pets — Libra Pets

Libra pets get along with each other. They will take turns rolling on top of each other when they play, neither ever attaining a dominant position. They play gently and quietly, and rarely become overactive or overexcited. Chasing each other wildly around the house is uncharacteristic of this match-up. They do well when left by themselves. Since they do not crave their owner's attention, you will be free to pursue other activities without their involvement in your every move. A cool, calm, and collected atmosphere in the home occurs when there are two Libras. There is even a tendency towards laziness between two Libra-born animals.

Libra Pets — Scorpio Pets

Scorpio and Libra will not do very many things together. Scorpio pets usually bully Libra pets around, and will prevent Libra from developing the intertwining relationship with family members that is characteristic of this animal sign. Scorpios are prone to aggressive, violent explosions when they are housed with mild-mannered Libras. A Libra-born cat doesn't stand a chance against a Scorpio-born dog. These differing sun signs are better off if they never meet.

Libra Pets — Sagittarius Pets

Sagittarius and Libra pets have lots of fun together. This combination may be hard for their owners to discipline or control and will almost certainly result in making their home a bit messy. But they love each other and are hard to separate. Sagittarius is always teasing Libra, but Libra is patient and enjoys it. When Sagittarius feels the urge to go traveling, Libra usually stays home. Sagittarians get into mischief when they are around Librans, but that is their normal behavior. These signs match up well for dogs and cats.

Libra Pets — Capricorn Pets

Capricorn pets and Libra pets are both easygoing and well-mannered. Capricorns dominate relationships with Libras. There is much competition for affection of family members between these two animal signs, though, so they don't do as well when housed together. As casual acquaintances Capricorn pets will smother Libra pets with affection. Libra will lie there and take all the licks and love bites Capricorn can offer. The role is rarely reversed. Capricorn will do the loving, not receive it.

Libra Pets — Aquarius Pets

There is never a dull moment in a home with this matchup. There is never any viciousness between the two, but the relationship will run the gamut from friendliness to enmity. They are always full of surprises. Aquarius pets are the instigators of activities with Libra pets. However, once they start playing, Libras become dominant. They will occasionally growl and snarl at each other. Libra usually comes out on top and then they get along just fine. Libra pets willingly accept the loving and tender actions directed at them from Aquarius pets.

Libra Pets — Pisces Pets

Pisces and Libra pets are both easygoing and gentle natured, but they don't get along very well. The efforts of Pisces to play and make friends with Libra are usually rejected. Pisces pets' accurate intuition picks up on this rejection and they will go off by themselves. There is even occasional aggressiveness between these two animal signs, uncharacteristic behavior for both. The astute memory of Pisces will document Libra's resistance for future encounters.

Libra Pets — Aries Pets

Libra pets are better accepted by Aries pets if they are young puppies or kittens. Libras love to play with the enthusiastic Aries. Aries pets feel the need to be dominant over Libra. Aries has to be first to get the handout from the table, first to be petted when you return home, and first out the door when you let the two outside. Libra and Aries occasionally irritate each other, but not to the extent of harmful fighting. For the most part they get along if the companionship isn't permanent.

Libra Pets — Taurus Pets

There will be little activity between pets in your home if they have the sun signs of Libra and Taurus. They get along well in a melancholy way; they just don't stimulate one another. In fact, there is a tendency toward laziness when these two signs are together. They are both content to lie around the house and be pampered by their owners. This pet pairing may seem boring, but it is predictable and trustworthy. You will have very few worries with Libra and Taurus pets in your home.

Libra Pets — Gemini Pets

Gemini pets sense an attentive audience when a Libra pet is around. Geminis love to bounce around, play, and perform for Libras. This pair is at its best and most active when there are people around. When they are left alone, Libra pets tire of the uncontrollable Gemini and Gemini pets often leave Libras home and wander off. This may bring on one of Libra's claustrophobic and destructive attacks. Libra and Gemini will let other animals join in their adventures and will eagerly accept most other animal additions to the household.

Libra Pets — Cancer Pets

Cancer pets are resistant to most animal additions to their home. Cancers are unresponsive to Libra attempts at making friends. Libra pets will usually withdraw and hide from Cancer-born pets. The only way these two signs get along is if Libra takes on the characteristics of the Cancer cohabitant. Libra will be a bit neurotic and unstable if you let this occur. There are frequent fights between Libra pets and Cancer pets, especially when first meeting.

Libra Pets — Leo Pets

This is a very active combination of sun signs and they bring out the best in each other. Libras have a settling effect on Leos and Leo's wandering is decreased significantly. Libra tames the over-aggressiveness sometimes found in Leo pets. Leo's enthusiasm for exploring and playing with children will stimulate Libra to join in. These two signs are very responsive to each other's actions. They make good companions for the family and for each other.

Libra Pets — Virgo Pets

Libra-born pets are usually unresponsive to Virgo pets. Libras do not usually fight with Virgos, but they ignore them. Libra does not take to the shyness and tenderness exhibited by Virgo. They prefer more interaction, such as with family members. Virgos often get the blame for deeds that were done by their Libra housemates. When you arrive home to find the plants knocked over and the carpet chewed, chances are the culprit was your Libra and not your Virgo pet. Virgo-born pets have a hard time expressing their personalities with Libra pets constantly overshadowing them.

9

The Strength of Many:

The
SCORPIO
Pet

October 24 — November 21

The Scorpio Personality

Scorpio pets are strong bodied and strong willed. They enjoy activities that require physical prowess. Being "rough and ready" is an essential part of their makeup. Scorpio pets' physical strength is matched by their inner strength.

It is hard to tell what Scorpio pets are thinking. They have a proud and assured look — not mean, but stern enough to make you think twice before approaching.

Likewise, their fellow creatures are a little uneasy or taken aback when Scorpios are around.

Scorpio-born pets have the ability to concentrate totally on the affair at hand. They dive singlemindedly into one goal, and will use all their physical and emotional talents to complete any task, assigned or chosen. Because Scorpios love to work and perform alone, they make excellent "only" pets.

Scorpio pets seem to live from day to day. Every new situation is taken as a challenge that has to be mastered. They love to be tested, and to prove themselves to you over and over. They rarely show signs of weakness when it comes to physically demanding activities. Scorpio's pride will be crushed if you force them to back down from a confrontation in which they could prove themselves.

Neither you nor your friends should try to "stare down" your Scorpio pet. Looking an animal directly in the eyes is an act of aggression, and if you don't look away, Scorpio's intense and fiery nature may manifest itself. It is best to look away and let your Scorpio pet think that another challenge has been conquered.

In the animal world, your Scorpio pet's companions will not be so willing to give in to the "Battle of the Eyes." You will no doubt have to intervene quickly to prevent heated Scorpio skirmishes. If you don't learn to recognize your Scorpio's boiling point, you will have real wars on your hands. Fighting to the death is not unheard of among Scorpio-born animals, and Scorpios usually win. This is not to say that all they do is fight, but be cautious when new acquaintances are around. There is definitely a violent and destructive side to many Scorpio pets' personalities.

Of course, the more positive side of a Scorpio's volatile personality is an intense loyalty to their carefully chosen friends. Scorpio friendships are few and far between, a reason why smaller families provide a more suitable environment for Scorpio pets.

Scorpios have keen memories. The interaction you have at an early age with a Scorpio will determine the type of relationship that will ensue for years. Kindness when you first acquire your little Scorpio will be repaid lifelong. Likewise, if you treat Scorpios cruelly, they may take their fighting stance and never, *ever* retreat.

Scorpio pets are very possessive. They are not accumulators of useless trash, but rather choose possessions with great deliberation and discrimination, and are very unwilling to part with their assets. The Scorpio pet is not wasteful. Every morsel of food will be utilized. Toys, once accepted, will be used frequently, and guarded carefully.

Strict obedience is hard to find among Scorpio-born pets. They will cooperate to the extent necessary for sharing your domicile, but they clearly have minds of their own,and just as clearly find ways to let you know exactly what they think. Scorpios want to do things their way, every time. Training is best accomplished by working around this trait via give and take — mostly giving in on your part. There is more than one way to approach any training problem, and the Scorpio pet usually prefers the unconventional.

There is a need for privacy and seclusion among Scorpios. They enjoy doing things on their own, even secretly. If you invade them during one of their private times, they will most certainly stop what they are doing and may even try to draw you away from their intimate retreat. Try not to disturb Scorpio pets during their quiet or intense moments. Do not drive them from their dens of seclusion. They will just seek out others. Take comfort that at least you will know where Scorpio is.

The planet Pluto influences Scorpio. There is a strong urge for Scorpio pets to propagate their species. In fact, male cats will spend most nights away from home in search of receptive mates. They will get into numerous fights that will require medical attention. Male Scorpio dogs, too, will travel miles. Once their single-mindedness fastens on the opposite sex, there is no recalling Scorpio. It may become necessary for you to neuter your Scorpio pet because this is usually the only way to curb such behavior. Also, if your Scorpio fights constantly, neutering will help.

The appearance of Scorpio pets projects strength and determination. They have heavily boned frames and are medium to tall for their species. Their skulls are large and wide between the ears, with penetrating, unwavering eyes. They have strong jaws with bulging cheek muscles. Dark, thick coats of fur with a mahogany or reddish tinge are common. Their movements are slow and steady. Nervousness and flightiness are uncommon. Scorpio's overall appearance is often called "brawny." Deep reds, blues, and grays are the best Scorpio colors.

Scorpios are born nature-lovers. As early as possible, expose them to the outdoors where they may frolic to their heart's content without fear of reprimands. Let them expend their energies outside and they will be less intensely dispositioned indoors. Scorpio pets need to know that their stored-up vitality can be released regularly outdoors, or they will release it in your home.

Scorpio-born pets need to be triumphant in order to remain confident and content. Scorpios are very physical and excel in sporting activities, especially when unhampered by other animals. But don't ask them to attempt feats unsuited to their natural abilities. They will keep trying to master the test, to prove themselves to you, and will be overcome with frustration. This will cause the destructive tendencies of Scorpio to surface.

As Scorpio pets age, they develop daily routines from which they never stray. They will not form new friendships or accept new additions to the household. This includes family members as well as pets. They are jealous until the end.

The Scorpio Parent

Scorpio pets do not make the best parents. They will nurture and care for their young adequately, but they will visibly lack tenderness and commitment. They are very stern parents, and will tolerate little commotion. Scorpio parents are quick to pick their young up by the scruff of the neck and shake them vigorously for the least disruption. The youngsters will not be injured but may be oppressed.

Scorpio parents may even become jealous if you shower their newborns with the affection formerly reserved for them. Keep reassuring your Scorpio parent of your love. It is not uncommon for Scorpio parents to abandon some or all of their young. Try not to upset their usual routine and leave them as secluded as possible while they are rearing their offspring.

The Young Scorpio

Have you ever come across a basketful of puppies or kittens left on the church steps? They were probably Scorpios. Scorpio young are often unwanted. If you should decide to raise one of the orphans, or any other Scorpio-born pet, be firm. Timid or shy owners are easy prey for developing Scorpios. Aggressiveness is in their nature, and they can put you on the defensive very easily. Discourage aggressive behavior early. Scorpio young enjoy wrestling and tug-of-war type games, but don't let them get out of hand. The playfulness can lead to vigorous fighting that becomes a habit.

Scorpio-born youngsters tend to be destructive. They will chew and demolish everything they can fit their strong jaws around. A washcloth thoroughly soaked in water and then frozen will satisfy much of their craving for chewing, and will save the family household goods.

One good point about young Scorpio pets is that they learn their acceptable boundaries quickly. If rooms or spaces are off-limits, removing them a few times from the forbidden area will get the message across.

The Scorpio pet becomes set in its ways early. The old saying, "You can't teach an old dog new tricks," suggests the difficulty of changing your Scorpio's habits. Don't let unwanted behavior go unchecked, but don't be severe in your reprimands; Scorpios never forget.

It is a good idea to let your little Scorpio pet find an area in the home where it is removed from the normal environmental stimuli. Then do not trespass on the hideaway or it will search for another. Scorpio pets love to play hermit.

Young Scorpios do not have excessively strong bonds between littermates. They seem glad to leave the original family and move on to a new one. They are jealous when they have to compete with other animals or family members. Scorpios do best when raised as "only" pets.

The Healthy Scorpio

Scorpios are vulnerable to reproductive-system problems. These may include:

- pyrometra, or infections of the uterus;
- vaginal hyperplasia — enlargement of the vaginal walls,
- priapism — constant exposure of the male genitals
- prostate infections and tumors,

- retained testicle, which may lead to tumor development as the male Scorpio ages. (Have the retained testicle removed to prevent this.)

The nose and throat are vulnerable as well in many Scorpios. Be alert for:

- chronic tonsillitis

- epistaxis — chronic bleeding from the nose

- tracheobronchitis, whose symptoms are similar to the common cold

The skeletal system in Scorpios is often delicate, and prone to anything from rickets to:

- growth problems associated with Scorpio's large bones

- osteochondritis, a condition which may lead to arthritis if not treated early

- hip dysplasia, which may eventually be crippling

Scorpio Summary

A true Scorpio is tenacious to the point of death and has a mind of its own. If you insist on strict obedience and a nature that is always happy-go-lucky, this sign is probably not right for you. But the owner who appreciates fierce loyalty to a select few and a singleminded determination will find just these qualities in the typical Scorpio pet.

Scorpio Pet Compatibilities

Scorpio-born pets fight with most animals of the other sun signs. Compatible companions for Scorpio are often difficult to find.

The only animal signs that Scorpios get along with for extended periods are Pisces and Sagittarius. Scorpios will share their home with these two signs.

Pets born under the sun signs of Capricorn, Aquarius, Aries, Taurus, Gemini, Cancer, and Virgo do well only as brief encounters.

Scorpios, Leos, and Libras are best avoided.

Scorpio Pets — Scorpio Pets

Scorpio pets are attracted to the challenge they sense from the stare of other Scorpios. Violence of a harmful nature usually results. Neither will give in to the other, and once the fight has started it won't stop until there is a definite winner. If they should meet again, another fight will ensue. The results may be different from their last encounter. Since Scorpios are intense rivals, you should keep them from ever meeting if possible.

Scorpio Pets — Sagittarius Pets

One of Scorpio's few friendships may be with a Sagittarius-born pet. Having a Sagittarius around will improve Scorpio's disposition. Scorpios eagerly join in the playful activities of Sagittarians. Scorpios even become less serious about proving themselves physically in every new situation. Sagittarius will take Scorpio on many traveling adventures, and Scorpio will not inhibit the carefree attitude of Sagittarius. Some Sagittarius traits will rub off on Scorpio.

Scorpio Pets — Capricorn Pets

Capricorns and Scorpios are resistant and stubborn with each other. Each tries to dominate the other, but they end up taking turns on top. They often run from or ignore each other. They will leave each other alone for extended periods of time. As they grow older together they respect each other's habits, but they never get overly involved in each other's company. Capricorns eventually come out on top because they usually outlive Scorpios. These two signs should not be made to live together.

Scorpio Pets — Aquarius Pets

Aquarius pets and Scorpio pets are nervous around each other. Each keeps a watchful eye on the other's activities. The unpredictable nature of Aquarius pets, coupled with Scorpio's urge to dominate, makes quarrels frequent between these two signs. Each fears the other, which provides a nervous stalemate at times, giving the outward appearance of friendship. This never lasts, so keep their meetings short.

Scorpio Pets — Pisces Pets

Pisces pets bring out the performer in Scorpio. Scorpio will be physically active but rarely aggressive toward the passive and attentive Pisces. Scorpio will even stimulate the normally shy Pisces into joining in the playful antics. Scorpio does not feel the urge to dominate Pisces by fighting. This relationship is relatively quiet when compared to most of Scorpio's encounters. Like Sagittarius pets, Pisces pets are a good influence on Scorpios.

Scorpio Pets — Aries Pets

Aries pets have strong enough dispositions to handle Scorpios. The fearlessness of Aries offsets the physical advantage of most Scorpios. This relationship is always active and energetic, with occasional eruptions of temper on both sides. Aries has a small edge in domination over Scorpio. Aries and Scorpio need to be separated for periods of time or they get in each other's way and will fight.

Scorpio Pets — Taurus Pets

Taurus pets and Scorpio pets stick together through thick and thin. They fight as much as they get along, but they stay. Taurus is very tolerant of Scorpio's temperament and some of this patience rubs off on Scorpio. Scorpio is bound to disrupt the usually good nature of Taurus. There are times when Scorpios won't let Taureans be until they fight. The two signs often feud over their bones and toys.

Scorpio Pets — Gemini Pets

The high-spirited Gemini pet and the Scorpio pet get into lots of mischief when they are together. Scorpio becomes frustrated when trying to catch the fleet Gemini. Gemini's pace is too rapid for Scorpio. Scorpio pets become jealous of the attention given Gemini pets in their presence. When these two are together in a room, hold on to the lamps and vases. They are sure to knock over all but the most stable furnishings as they chase each other around.

Scorpio Pets — Cancer Pets

Scorpio-born pets are too aggressive and physical for intuitive, docile Cancer pets. The normally quiet Cancer will even fight when a Scorpio enters the home. Cancer loses the battle and is dominated and abused by Scorpio. There is much jealousy between these two signs.

Scorpio Pets — Leo Pets

Fierce battles and utter chaos result when these two sun signs are brought together. There is a constant struggle for the dominant position. Leo pets become very vocal and will bark, howl, or meow ferociously when Scorpio pets are around. Neither Leo nor Scorpio will completely give in to the other. It is best to keep them in separate rooms if they have to be in the same home.

Scorpio Pets — Virgo Pets

Unless they are forced to live together, Virgo pets and Scorpio pets get along well. The good points of both come out when they are casual acquaintances. Scorpio is lively, entertaining, and physical. Virgo is compassionate, tender, and shy. They will not compete for the affection of people around them. When kept together for extended periods, Scorpios will become aggressive toward Virgos. Dogs and cats of differing Scorpio and Virgo signs are almost always enemies.

Scorpio Pets — Libra Pets

Scorpio pets and Libra pets will not do many things together. Scorpio pets usually bully Libra pets around, appear to be intensely jealous, and prevent Libra from developing the intertwining relationship with family members that is character-istic of this animal sign. Scorpios are prone to aggressive, violent explosions when they are housed with mild-mannered Libras. A Libra-born cat doesn't stand a chance against a Scorpio-born dog. These differing sun signs are better off if they never meet.

10

Have Fun, Will Travel:

The
SAGITTARIUS
Pet

November 22 — December 21

The Sagittarius Personality

Sagittarius-born pets, ruled by the planet Jupiter, are inquisitive, friendly, happy, fun-loving...and surprisingly shy. They aren't fearful, just a bit cautious with new company, but they soon learn to mask their shyness as cuteness. The pet that makes you say "Awww" is likely a Sag.

Sagittarius pets, the greatest travelers in the zodiac, absolutely must feel free. You will no doubt have trouble with your Sagittarian's desire to wander. Their lives can become devoted to seeking out new adventures. They like to keep on the move in the fresh air. They are easily bored, and if their lives aren't busy enough at home, they won't hesitate to look for a change of scenery. They always return after their investigative urges are satisfied, but are sometimes gone for days. And, just as Sagittarius pets need freedom to roam, so they require freedom from strict rules. They won't follow arbitrary commands: you won't be able to make them do tricks just for your pleasure, or to entertain others. The Sagittarian's free spirit is not available for harnessing. They love outdoor activities and will readily retrieve, swim, and hunt, but absolutely, positively won't roll over and play dead. Or shake hands. Or bark or meow on cue.

Sagittarius pets are known for developing friendships with the neighbors and their pets. It is not unusual for them to have a home away from home. Sagittarians are very often taken in as strays while they are on an excursion. They love to play with children, and children love them. If you are out searching for your little travel bug, talk to the local kids. You'll probably find out that your Sagittarius pet has spent considerable time, perhaps even days, at everyone's house but yours and is answering eagerly to a new name. When you retrieve your unrepentant wanderer, tell its hosts not to worry; it will find its way back, usually soon.

There isn't much you can do to subdue the wanderlust. Locking up your Sagittarius will break its carefree spirit. As it ages, though, its wandering will decrease. Once it has thoroughly investigated all that life has to offer, it will take its ease at home.

Sagittarius pets will often bring other animals home. They know you don't like their being gone all the time, and their enthusiastic and playful natures inspire other animals to follow them.

Sagittarius pets have lots of stamina. Their energy is boundless, and they are tireless travelers. When they eventually return home, they will very often sleep for two or three days. Once they recuperate, keep them active and interested or they may disappear again.

Sagittarius pets are good-natured and loving. They will not intentionally harm people or other animals. However, they do not back down from fights if challenged.

If you take your Sagittarius visiting with you, be prepared for something unexpected. Sagittarians have a way of embarrassing you or your friends. Investigating under the couch or elsewhere, they may produce unexplainable artifacts. They are also good at knocking things over with their tails and paws.

Sagittarius pets are rarely mean. They have a high tolerance for kidding and abuse. They are not possessive of their playthings or friends (human or otherwise), and are safe around children of all ages. Kids are always coming up with new games and novel ideas to keep Sagittarians interested and active.

When Sagittarius pets become enthusiastic over one thing, they easily forget other basics. They forget the car window is rolled up and try to hop through it. They forget where they buried their last bone because they were so excited about doing it. Sagittarius cats may forget there is a window between them and the bird flying by. They are among the more intelligent animals of their kind, but at times seem to lack common sense. Their impulsiveness can put them in awkward situations.

Sagittarius pets trust people. They remain naive all their lives. They will readily hop into a stranger's car, and are easy to play tricks on until the novelty wears off.

You can be firm when disciplining your Sagittarius pet. They seem unconcerned over mild discipline and will go right back to what they were doing in the first place. They don't hold grudges or stay depressed.

Due to Sagittarians' restless nature, they do better in homes with lots of room to explore and wander outdoors. If kept in apartments, they will leave often and may seek a larger home to settle in. They love their owners, but won't think twice if it comes down to deciding between you or their freedom.

If you have to move your family to another home, your Sagittarius pet will have no trouble adapting. It enjoys new experiences in new areas. In fact, if your life-style requires constant moves, your Sagittarius will be delighted.

Many Sagittarius pets are little daredevils. They fear nothing, and will follow their owners and friends anywhere. They will jump off ladders into swimming pools. They will walk onto floating logs. They would skydive out of a plane if you went first. Such is their trust in mankind, and such is Sagittarius bravery.

Sagittarius pets love nature and the outdoors and do well in a variety of climates. Extremes in hot or cold will not affect their robustness. The dogs make excellent hunters, and the cats make excellent mousers.

Physically, Sagittarius pets appear tall, but are actually of medium height for the breed. Their bones are of medium thickness, covered with well-defined lean musculature. They feel firm to the touch. Their teeth are usually large and straight. Many of them have a prominent arch on their nose. They don't have thick coats, but rather fine fur. If they are born light-colored, their fur will darken with age. If they are born dark-colored, they often lighten in color with age. Their movements are quick.

Sagittarius pets keep their enthusiastic and friendly nature to the end. Their roaming and adventurousness will decrease and they will stay closer to home as they grow older. They do not become unresponsive to their owners, nor do they develop other senile changes commonly seen in dogs and cats. They love to be sneaked up on and surprised, even in their geriatric years.

The Sagittarius Parent

Sagittarius pets make adequate parents. When the young are first born they are not as affectionate as other parents. Any troubles with rearing their young will appear in the first few days after birth. As the youngsters age, the Sagittarius parent will become more involved, clearly preferring buddies rather than a bunch of babies.

The Young Sagittarius

Sagittarius pets keep their early personalities throughout their lives. They never seem to grow up. They are always happy, playful, and eager to join in games. They desire companions and will seek out crowds rather than remain alone.

Sagittarius is easily trained in the basics such as litterbox use. They love to be rewarded for their efforts; in fact they seem to expect it. They are easily bored and distracted, so make the training sessions short, fun, and rewarding. Young Sagittarians will not stick to regular routines of eating and going outside. They prefer to do things their way and when they feel like it. You will have to accommodate their untimely demands if you wish their training to progress rapidly. You can change the time and order of doing things when they get older; they are receptive to change and can adapt readily.

Young Sagittarius pets are always in places they shouldn't be, due to their inquisitive nature. You should watch them carefully until they are older, because many young Sagittarians get hurt by being in the wrong place at the wrong time. Falls from high places are also common in these fearless youngsters. At times they can be a bit reckless.

You will probably have a kitchen full of different puppy or kitten foods for Sagittarius pets. They aren't finicky, they just get bored with the same diet. Don't throw any pet foods away, just rotate them. What little Sagittarians won't eat today, they may eat tomorrow or the next day.

The Healthy Sagittarius

Muscles and bones are Sagittarian susceptibilities.

- Hip displasia may require surgery or may result in crippling arthritis later; rheumatoid-type arthritis in all joints is also common.

The area around the tail and flanks should be carefully watched.

- Perianal adenoma and tumors under the tail and around the rear end are frequent in male Sagittarius dogs. Surgery, castration, or hormonal therapy is needed for treatment.

- Rectal fistulas are also found in this sun sign, and are very difficult to treat.

- Anal gland infections and abscesses may require surgical removal.

Liver problems may plague Sagittarius, too.

- Hepatitis may be caused from another primary illness. (Be sure to vaccinate for the preventable hepatitis.)

- Heartworms can cause liver damage; watch also for tumors on the liver and spleen.

- Bloodstream problems include several auto-immune diseases that cause anemia and sometimes jaundice, as well as systemic lymphosarcoma, a malignant cancer of the lymph nodes which may cause visible swellings on the back of the thighs.

- Mild respiratory infections should always be treated immediately, as a seemingly minor condition can quickly develop into serious pneumonia.

Sagittarius Summary

You will need a large home or lots of space to give the Sagittarius pet the optimum setting. You must also be willing to offer much more freedom than is usual. If you can do these things for the Sagittarius pet, you will be rewarded with a friendly, affectionate, and playful addition to the household.

Sagittarius Pet Compatibilities

Adventuresome Sagittarius pets are known for getting along with other animals and with children. They bring a playful attitude to many relationships.

The most compatible signs for Sagittarius pets in the home are Capricorn, Pisces, Aries, Taurus, Gemini, Leo, Libra, Scorpio, and other Sagittarians.

The combination of Virgo or Aquarius with Sagittarius is troublesome over any long period.

Cancer pets make the least desirable companions for Sagittarius pets.

Sagittarius Pets — Sagittarius Pets

There will be lots of action and excitement with this combination. They have fun with each other indoors and out. Tempers flare occasionally between the two, but not to the extent of causing harm to each other. They share a mutual desire to wander and frequently run away from home. They don't become jealous if their owners take only one for a car ride or show affection to one and not the other.

Sagittarius Pets — Capricorn Pets

Sagittarius will bring out the playfulness in Capricorn pets. Both will be interested and eager to join in the other one's activities. They enjoy each other's company and are difficult to separate. Capricorn will help to keep Sagittarius pets from straying. Capricorn will become jealous of Sagittarius if you aren't careful in showing affection. Often you will have to favor the Capricorn so it will feel equally loved.

Sagittarius Pets — Aquarius Pets

This pairing of signs is occasionally volatile. Especially between dogs and cats of these two signs, fighting occurs. The Aquarius pet will become overly enthusiastic when attempting to join in with the Sagittarian's activities, often following Sagittarius around like a shadow and sticking their noses where they aren't wanted. A quick snap by Sagittarius sends the Aquarius pet on its way.

Sagittarius Pets — Pisces Pets

Pisces-born pets are receptive toward Sagittarius pets' advances. They eagerly join in the freewheeling activities of Sagittarius and will even become more adventurous. It is not unusual for Pisces to go on an uncharacteristic trip away from home with the traveling Sagittarius. Pisces pets are the initiators of tender moments between the two and these moments last but a short time. The abundant enthusiasm in Sagittarius pets will overflow into Pisces and make them happier and more active.

Sagittarius Pets — Aries Pets

Sagittarius pets will get their own way with Aries pets, but they will not dominate Aries physically. Aries loves to play tricks on Sagittarians and is always hiding and sneaking up on them. Aries and Sagittarius will share many travels. They always want to go outside and are a difficult pair to keep indoors or at home. If you take Aries and Sagittarius on vacation or visiting with you, they may disappear for hours. Aries pets and Sagittarius pets have endless fun with one another.

Sagittarius Pets — Taurus Pets

Taurus and Sagittarius pets get along with each other without too much commotion, although they don't interact much or share many activities. Neither will restrict the other one's personality; they will live and let live. Taurus is content to watch Sagittarius' antics and will not follow on those frequent excursions from home. Taurus doesn't try to keep up with Sagittarius and Sag doesn't try to coax Taurus along.

Sagittarius Pets — Gemini Pets

These signs complement each other. They are always on the go together and are equally matched in stamina and endurance. They will play together, and they will play by themselves. They leave each other alone as much as they are together, but they are difficult to keep at home. Gemini pets and Sagittarius pets do not compete for their owner's affections or even for food or toys.

Sagittarius Pets — Cancer Pets

These two sun signs should never meet. The Cancer-born pet prefers to stay home and the Sagittarius pet prefers to leave. Sagittarius will always be running away from home if a Cancer pet is there. If they are locked in the same home together, Sagittarius will be anything but affectionate to Cancer. There will be much fighting on a vocal level. Growling, snarling, and hissing abounds in homes unfortunate enough to have a Sagittarius-Cancer pet combination.

Sagittarius Pets — Leo Pets

Animals of these signs have great fun together. Sagittarius will be the more active, causing Leo to quicken its usually strolling pace. This twosome often becomes active during the night. When they are out on the town, Leo will let Sagittarius do the initial exploring and take all the chances, often acting as lookout and warning Sagittarius of danger.

Sagittarius Pets — Virgo Pets

Virgo pets and Sagittarius pets, dogs and cats alike, enjoy playing together. Often Sagittarius will not finish the game or activity they start together, leaving Virgo bewildered. They don't do as well when they are constantly together in the same home, as Sagittarius often abandons Virgo in the midst of Virgo's happiness and excitement. This will eventually make the Virgo pet reluctant to show its affection towards the Sag and other household inhabitants. When the relationship is kept casual, Virgo will romp and play with the Sagittarius pet like a puppy or a kitten. Keep a close eye on your Virgo pet when you let them out to play with the neighbor's Sagittarian, as Virgo is very likely to follow the wanderer on an extended excursion.

Sagittarius Pets — Libra Pets

Sagittarius and Libra pets are very well paired. This combination may be hard for their owners to discipline or control and will certainly make your home a bit messy. But they love each other and are hard to separate. Sagittarius pets are always teasing Libra pets, but Libra is patient and enjoys it. When Sagittarius feels the urge to go traveling, Libra usually stays home. Sagittarius pets get into lots of mischief around Libra pets, but that is their normal behavior and keeps them happy. You will have two cheerful, playful animals with Libra and Sagittarius in your home. These signs also match up well for dogs and cats.

Sagittarius Pets — Scorpio Pets

One of Scorpio's few friends may be a Sagittarius. Having a Sagittarius pet will improve tough Scorpio's disposition. Scorpios will eagerly join in the playful activities of Sagittarians, and will become less serious about proving themselves physically in every new situation. Sagittarius will take Scorpio traveling. Scorpio will not inhibit the carefree attitude of the Sagittarius pet. Some Sagittarius traits will rub off on Scorpio.

11

Forever Young:

The
CAPRICORN
Pet

December 22 — January 19

The Capricorn Personality

Easygoing Capricorn pets are a little on the shy side, even a bit withdrawn. They like to observe a new situation for a while before mingling, and tend to hold back vocally as well. Capricorn-born pets will not bark just to hear their own voices and will not keep you up all night meowing. When they bark or meow, there is a reason...and it's usually a complaint. Strongly committed and loyal to their owners, Capricorns are predictable and consistent in all responses. However, Capricorn pets do get "the blues" regularly; at times, the term "sourpuss" seems invented just for them.

Capricorn pets tend to live far beyond anyone's expectations. Even your pet's veterinarian will be surprised at your Capricorn's longevity. This is worth noting, for when your pet reaches geriatric age you may be faced with major medical decisions. It is always worth treating the older Capricorn pet's medical problems, even if the prognosis is poor. Capricorn pets, both cats and dogs, have a full "nine lives" to draw upon. They rebound from illnesses in the face of all odds.

Your Capricorn pet thrives on praise. You must be very eager to show outward, physical approval for even the smallest deeds well done. This will help to keep the pet's behavior consistent, which is basic to its nature. Your Capricorn pet will readily develop a daily routine aimed at eliciting your praise.

The Capricorn pet prefers quiet, familiar surroundings. This is not to say that you shouldn't have people or other animals over to your house. Your Capricorn's cautious side will become apparent when this occurs, but it will soon find acceptable ways to blend in. You can feel safe to take it visiting with you. Capricorn pets will rarely cause embarrassment to their owners. Just be sure to give them reassurance that their normal behavior is noticed and appreciated.

Capricorns will submit willingly to their owner's requests. They are not stubborn (flexibility of temperament being one of their strong points) once they determine what type of behavior is acceptable to their owners. You must be patient, however, for Capricorns are slow learners. They have a lot of persistence and training sessions can last much longer than with other animals. Methodical and precise in their movements and thoughts, Capricorns will eventually achieve what is asked of them. Lavish them with praise along the way, and although they are plodders, the extra time that you can spend with them will result in advancements in the training.

Capricorn cats are avid climbers. They have a strong desire to perch in high places so they can observe everything going on around them. A cat that loves to ride or sit on your shoulder is very likely a Capricorn. This sign will pick the highest accessible point in any room as a lookout tower. They have an excellent sense of balance and will often be seen tightrope-walking along fences, poles, and even large wires.

Capricorn felines have the reputation of being all claws. When you pick them up they always climb up (and snag) your sweater to reach your shoulder or head. At Christmastime, they feel compelled to climb to the top of the delicately decorated tree. Many Capricorn cat owners ask to have their pets declawed. If little Capricorn is strictly an indoor inhabitant, there is nothing wrong with this minor surgical procedure. But if your pet is to spend any time outdoors, you will be removing their major tool of defense and retreat.

As Capricorn cats are driven to climbing, so Capricorn dogs are driven to digging. They master the art of excavation early. This is a difficult habit to break and you will have better luck in redirecting it than in stopping it. I have even had desperate owners ask me to declaw Capricorn dogs. This is, of course, a drastic measure and is avoidable if you will do the following.

Designate one area in the corner of the yard, or elsewhere, as the mining area. Allow digging here and discourage it in other areas. The placing of mothballs in small holes where undesirable digging takes place will help to keep your

Capricorn pet in the assigned area. Also save cigarette butts, cigar butts, or other tobacco and put it in the ends of old nylons. Hang these "digging repellents" on your fragile bushes or plants to prevent their destruction. Your Capricorn pet will soon get the point.

Capricorns are among the best animal playmates for a young child. They will retain their puppyish or kittenish playfulness throughout adulthood, giving them a natural rapport with children.

The stamina and endurance found in Capricorn-born pets enable them to play endlessly with children. They won't be the ones to tire first. They have a reverence for family members and a harmless disposition towards them. You need not worry about play becoming too rough. A word of caution, though, if you have an extremely large Capricorn pet as a playmate for an infant. While they have no tendency toward viciousness, they may not know their own strength when playing with fragile babies. Even the kindest of nudges from a large, playful Capricorn can topple a toddler who has just learned to walk.

You can trust your Capricorn pet at home alone. The worst that will happen is they will be gloomy when you return. They are not destructive and have an inborn discipline over their aggressiveness.

The Capricorn pet also has an abundance of patience — which is rare in the animal kingdom. When asked to sit or stay, it will remain in that position contentedly until you call it away. When you are opening a favorite food, it will not leap all over you, but calmly wait for what is obviously coming.

Have you lost a ring, your favorite trinket, or a child's small toy? If any of them were left on the floor or outside, the Capricorn pet would think nothing of swallowing it. Capricorns tend to have an abnormal craving for unusual objects. Many a Capricorn X-ray has shown a stomach like a hardware store.

The Capricorn pet will never be seen pulling their owners down the sidewalk at the end of a leash. They're even content to let you led. They seem to know that they will reach their destination the same time as you, whether they act like fools or not. Capricorn pets are surefooted; clumsiness and awkwardness are not in their makeup.

Capricorn pets love to take their owners with them on their adventures. They may be patiently sitting at the door for you to let them outside, then when you open the door they continue to sit there looking eagerly at you. This is an invitation to come out and play. It will be hard to resist their childlike offer.

Physically, Capricorn pets are usually slender. They tend to have long bodies or long legs. Their bone structure is thin, and this is especially evident in their faces and heads, which are long and narrow. They usually have dark fur that is straight and long, often the darkest of red for their breed. There is a preponderance of small eyes, which are usually dark. Their teeth are prominent, pearl-white, and healthy. The best colors for Capricorn pets are dark blues, browns, and black.

Care must be taken when bathing your Capricorn pet. It will have sensitive skin, and itching and flaking may result from bathing. Use bath oil (such as Alpha-Keri) for rinsing to prevent this.

The Capricorn Parent

As parents, Capricorn-born pets adore their young. They act more like siblings than parents to their offspring. They will enjoy sharing in all of their little ones' playful antics, and make rearing their young a pleasure.

When it comes times for your Capricorn to have her puppies, keep a close eye on her when you let her outside. I have known expectant Capricorns to dig dens in which to whelp their pups, just as a fox or wolf would do. If you allow her to do this, you will not see the offspring for weeks until they are able to crawl out of their underground nest. They will be safe and secure, even if it is winter, but you will be unable to lend a helping hand if it is needed.

The Young Capricorn

It is easy to spot a litter of Capricorn puppies or kittens. They look like miniature adults of their breed. They retain their appearance throughout their lives. What you see is what you get with the Capricorn-born youngster. Don't expect them to grow into something different.

Capricorn youngsters tend to be quiet. They are not whiners and will not keep you up all night crying. They move about slowly and deliberately. They tend to be cautious. The young Capricorn pet is an amazing climber. You will find them on top of everything, although they are very submissive to their owners.

Give the Capricorn puppy or kitten a little toy and it will be guarded like a treasure. It will become their security blanket.

They tend to mind their own business and will not stick their little noses where they are not wanted.

The new Capricorn pet adapts to routine feedings and subsequent house training. If you keep to a regular feeding schedule, rather than having food available constantly, it will be easier to house or litterbox train them. You can expect them to have to go within minutes after feeding, so put them outside or in their litterbox immediately and don't let them leave the area until they have done their duties. If you will also take them out once in between feedings, you will have them house trained in no time.

Remember that Capricorn-born pets learn slowly, so be patient and persistent. They take their sweet time and concentrate deeply on every move. The more experience they have, the better they will become. They will remain like puppies or kittens throughout their entire lives.

The Healthy Capricorn

A close eye on Capricorn's skeletal system is always smart. Be alert for signs of arthritis (hip dysplasia, arthritis in the knees, elbows, and shoulders, and especially fractures of the legs and bone tumors).

Skin is sensitive in Capricorns, too. They're very vulnerable to allergies — seasonal itching, flea allergy, and other allergies. It may be better in the long run to have your young Capricorn pet allergy-tested rather than to rely on prolonged and frequent use of Cortisone to control the itching and self-mutilation. Always use an oil rinse after bathing Capricorn pets.

Capricorn pets are prone to pica, or an abnormal craving for substances unfit as food. They may ingest unusual objects or even their own stools. Your veterinarian can help your Capricorn pet with these problems. Stomach upsets may be the result of Capricorn's pica abnormality.

The chest is another vulnerable Capricorn spot. Chest problems in Capricorn cats include feline infectious peritonitis in the chest cavity, and pneumonia. The pneumonia problems can usually be prevented with annual vaccinations. Tumors in the lungs are seen in many Capricorns, too — as lymphosarcoma in Capricorn cats, a variety of tumors in Capricorn dogs, especially tumors of the ribs, or (in Capricorn females) tumors of the mammary glands.

Capricorn Summary

If you are looking for an obedient pet, one that will play with the kids and live to a ripe old age, Capricorn is for you. You will need some extra time, patience, and affection when you first acquire little Capricorn, so be prepared.

Capricorn Pet Compatibilities

Capricorn-born pets are cautious when meeting other animals. Fighting is not one of their vices and they will find a way to blend in with even the more aggressive signs.

Capricorn pets have very few problems when sharing their home with Aries, Leo, Virgo, Sagittarius, Aquarius, or other Capricorns.

Pets with the sun signs of Pisces, Taurus, Gemini, Cancer, Libra, or Scorpio make fine occasional companions for Capricorn pets.

There are no animal sun signs that have to be avoided for the accommodating Capricorn pet.

Capricorn Pets — Capricorn Pets

Mutual caution makes this relationship slow to form. The two will keep their distance from each other at first, then gradually enter one another's territory and become friends. Fights are unheard of, even between Capricorn dogs and Capricorn cats. Both Capricorns will be very quiet, even quieter than when they are by themselves. They will remain independent of each other. They don't have to always tag along to see what the other is doing. Your home life will be quiet and uneventful (bordering on dull) if you have two Capricorn pets.

Capricorn Pets — Aquarius Pets

Capricorn pets and Aquarius pets are calm and respectful of each other, although a bit noisy when people or other animals come around. They stay together most of the time and are well mannered in each other's presence. Capricorn is very patient with the aggressiveness shown toward them by the inquisitive Aquarius. Aquarius pets are constantly poking and prodding relaxing Capricorn pets, but will respect Capricorn's subtle growl or nip.

Capricorn Pets — Pisces Pets

Capricorn pets will become dominant over the submissive Pisces pet. Pisces will be outwardly affectionate toward Capricorn. Capricorn does not return all the licks and nibbles that they receive from Pisces. This pet partnership does best when there are children around to interact with both. Pisces pets do not receive the attention they need from Capricorn pets. When these two signs are kept together in the same house, Capricorn rules the day and Pisces becomes active during the night while Capricorn is sleeping.

Capricorn Pets — Aries Pets

This is a happy, playful, and entertaining pairing of signs. The high-spirited Aries pet will initiate most of the activities between the two. Capricorn is happy to join in the playfulness to the finish. Aries tends to dominate the relationship, but Capricorn is happy and emotionally stable. When Capricorn tries to initiate play, Aries is stubborn and may not start playing until it appears Capricorn has given up. Aries pets can be a bit snappy with Capricorn pets, but it rarely leads to fighting. Capricorn and Aries blend best as two-dog or two-cat relationships. Capricorn dogs and Aries cats do not mix very well.

Capricorn Pets — Taurus Pets

These two animal signs are stubborn with each other's advances when they first meet. It takes time for Capricorn is slow to give in, but they eventually get along well. Neither will become wild or uncontrollable when the other is around. They will both listen to and follow their owner's commands. Capricorn pets will try only once to take away the Taurus's bones or toys, quickly learning to respect the other's possessions. They both love to play with children, will not fight for their attention or affection, and are safe to have together around children.

Capricorn Pets — Gemini Pets

The Gemini pet is too active for Capricorn's easygoing nature. They get along well for short periods of time, then Capricorn tires of Gemini's relentless disturbances. It will be difficult to control either the Capricorn pet or the Gemini pet when the two are together. If this pair is kept together too long, Capricorn will reject all of Gemini's playful advances. The Gemini pet will then become frantic and try to involve whoever else is around.

Capricorn Pets — Cancer Pets

Cancer-born pets are attracted to Capricorn pets. They don't seem to be able to leave the irresistible Capricorn alone. They will be affectionate towards each other when they meet only occasionally and only for short periods. If they are housed together, the Cancer pet will not take its eyes off the Capricorn, will refuse to share its home with Capricorn, and will let Capricorn have no peace or quiet. Every move Capricorn makes is then watched and usually opposed by Cancer. They should not be kept in the same household if at all possible.

Capricorn Pets — Leo Pets

This is a good combination. Both Leos and Capricorns will be themselves. Capricorn will be excited by Leo's carefree and assertive nature. Leo will feel like the King, although the kingdom will be limited by Capricorn. Capricorn will be able to live in peace in a space separate from the King's. With Leo around, Capricorn becomes more outgoing and more vocal. Each takes on a carefree and happy disposition in the other's presence. A Leo cat and a Capricorn dog make a constantly entertaining pair.

Capricorn Pets — Virgo Pets

Virgo pets and Capricorn pets complement each other in a household. There will not be much barking or meowing in your home with these two. They will play together for hours. They are very affectionate toward each other and will lie around in the evenings licking and cleaning one another's fur. Breeding builds the affectionate bond between Virgo pets and Capricorn pets and they will be content to stay home with each other. Fighting between these signs is rare, even between cats and dogs.

Capricorn Pets — Libra Pets

Capricorn pets and Libra pets are both easygoing and well mannered. Capricorn dominates the relationships. There is much competition for the affection of family members between these two, so they don't do as well with each other when housed together. On casual acquaintance, Capricorn pets will smother Libra pets with affection. Libra will lie there and take all the licks and love bites Capricorn can offer. The role is rarely reversed. Capricorn will do the loving, not receive it. It is difficult for owners to keep both of these affection-craving signs happy in the same household.

Capricorn Pets — Scorpio Pets

Capricorn and Scorpio pets are resistant and stubborn with each other. Each tries to dominate the other, but they end up taking turns on top. They often run away from or quietly ignore each other. They will leave one another alone for extended periods. As they grow older together, they respect each other's habits, but they never get overly involved in each other's company. Capricorns may eventually come out on top because they usually outlive Scorpios. These two signs should not be made to live together.

Capricorn Pets — Sagittarius Pets

Sagittarius will bring out the playfulness in Capricorn pets. Both will be interested and eager to join in the other's activities. They enjoy each other's company and are difficult to separate. Capricorn will help to keep Sagittarius pets from straying from home. Capricorn pets will become jealous of Sagittarius pets if you're not careful when showing them affection. Often you will have to favor Capricorn pets to make them feel they have gotten their fair share of attention.

12

A Different Drummer:

The
AQUARIUS
Pet

January 20 — February 18

The Aquarius Personality

Aquarius-born pets are full of surprises. "Strange," "crazy," "goofy," and "loony" are typical owners' remarks about their Aquarian cats and dogs. "Free spirited" is a kinder description, and just as true.

You can never accurately predict what Aquarian pets will do. They rarely react the same way twice to a given situation. This may be due in part to their poor memories. The next time friends try to show you their pet's latest trick and the little beast just sits there dumbfounded, tell them it's not their fault, but the Aquarian influence. Pets of this sign are by no means unintelligent; they're just a bit scatterbrained and *very* charming! Aquarians are vivacious and friendly to everyone, even other animals. They have an innate curiosity that often leads them into trouble, and they may act impulsively, with a quick but harmless temper.

Aquarian pets always go their own way, and often do not conform to what is considered normal for their breed. Because of this, they sometimes don't live up to their owners' expectations.

The Aquarian-born pet is not one to be jealous of other animals or humans. Feel free to show affection to others in your pet's presence. Its feelings will not be hurt.

Aquarians do not take orders willingly. They can become very stubborn when you dish out commands. The more you try to force them to do things, the worse the situation becomes. It is not unusual for the disinterested Aquarian to turn around and simply run off in the middle of your increasingly insistent requests, nor is it unusual for Aquarian pets to calmly ignore their owners' comments, commands, and pleas. They will just lie there and not wink an eye. If this behavior becomes frequent, owners may even think there is something wrong with the pets' hearing. I have had clients bring in their Aquarians to be examined for deafness. After the physical examination is over, I usually end up explaining that this is just part of the indifferent Aquarian nature.

Aquarian pets have an urge to inspect every new nook and cranny, and inquisitive Aquarians stick their noses in the most unlikely spots.

Aquarian-born cats, for instance, will learn at an early age how to open your kitchen cupboards. They will enter the enticing little "caves" and proceed to inspect all contents. They may even throw a few articles down to the curious canine Aquarian waiting anxiously below. (I speak from experience.)

Don't let Aquarian pets see you hide anything from them. They will not rest easy until they have exhausted all possible means of getting their paws on it. If an Aquarian pet has an affinity for a certain object, toy, or such, leave it out in the open where the pet can see it, but not reach it, which satisfies that Aquarian curiosity and lets the pet settle down.

When visitors come to your house, they will no doubt have to be inspected by your Aquarian inhabitant. Nothing is off limits when the Aquarian pet's sniffer goes into action.

Likewise, if you take your inquisitive Aquarian visiting with you, expect it to check out the new premises with all the efficiency of a bomb squad. Until your friends and neighbors come to know your Aquarian pet's personality, they may often refer to your little friend as a pest.

Aquarian pets will not hold a grudge against you if reprimanding them becomes necessary. They forgive and forget. It is a good thing this is true since the uncooperative Aquarius nature requires frequent disciplining.

One thing I can say on behalf of Aquarians is that they are interesting and original. As a veterinarian I have just about seen and heard it all, except when a client tells me about an Aquarian pet's adventures.

Aquarian pets need to feel free. They need the freedom to explore and the freedom to rest. They take well to nature, especially water, and much of their inquisitive energy can be expelled in this harmless environment.

Aquarian-born pets have short spells in which they seem to go into hibernation. "Do Not Disturb" are the words to remember when this occurs. They will make all sorts of grumbling noises if you upset them during periods of tranquility. They will seek another secluded hideout if their sanctuary is disrupted.

Aquarian pets mingle well with crowds of people as well as other animals. They will bounce around from one person to the next, as if they belonged to everybody. They may not even claim you when you call them.

Aquarian pets are not ones to shower their owners with outward signs of affection. They will wag their tails or purr when happy, but are not ones to give you wet kisses or cuddle with you for hours on the couch. They seem to almost lack emotion.

Aquarian pets are fascinated by young children. Their playful antics are perceived as cute by children, and are encouraged. This is unlike most of their adult confrontations in which their behavior may be discouraged. Aquarians are unable to resist the calls of exuberant children. They are attracted like bees to honey.

Aquarian pets will never try to hide their unpredictable follies. Good or bad, their behavior is always out in the open for everyone to see. They do things by impulse, on the spur of the moment, never remembering the probable consequences. Aquarian pets often forget what behavior is acceptable and what is not. They don't have a strong sense of right and wrong, so you can't blame them for what they do.

It's hard (close to impossible, actually) to develop any sort of reliable routine with an Aquarius. Your Aquarian pet will try out different areas in your home for nighttime sleeping. They will not designate one specific area or one piece of furniture as their regular sleeping quarters. They will spend one week by the basement door, another week next to your bed, and the next week who knows where. Don't be offended if they vacate their previous bed when you have just covered it with your specially made afghan.

Aquarian pets are among the most vocal you can find. They may even develop a knack to utter sounds that resemble words. Dogs will bark at the least little stimulus and cats will cry like babies. They seem to like hearing their own voices. If you have to leave your Aquarian pet in a kennel, don't be surprised if its voice is hoarse when you return.

Aquarian pets make friends easily with most of the neighborhood animals. They are willing to share their possessions and may donate a bone or two for the friendship.

You can feel safe if little children are playing with your Aquarian pets' food or toys. They are not possessive by nature and taking a toy or bone away from them will not incite their aggressiveness.

Cold weather disagrees with most Aquarian pets, especially cats. When you open the door for them to go outside and they stick a little paw into the freshly fallen snow, they will retreat indoors and not want to go back out until spring. You should force the Aquarian dog to go outside when the weather is cold. It will keep it healthier in the long run. Don't worry about its feeling the cold.

Physically, Aquarian pets are a little on the tall side. Their musculature makes them look physically fit, but a bit awkward. Their fur is usually straight, soft, and blonde or light brown in color. They have large wide heads with blue or gray eyes. Their heads often bob when they walk. Blue, green, and purple are the colors of Aquarius.

The Aquarius Parent

Aquarian pets will be better parents if you wait until they are older to breed. They need to live their lies of impatience, independence, and impulsiveness. They are easily detached from their offspring, spending more time than usual away from the nest and their parental duties. They are not overly affectionate to their young and are impatient to the little ones' demands. You may find yourself bottle-feeding a litter of puppies or kittens if you mate your Aquarian pet too soon. Neutering the Aquarian may be doing it a favor.

The Young Aquarius

Aquarian puppies or kittens are real live wires. You will have your hands full with the independent and curious baby Aquarian. At their best, they are amusing and cute. At their worst, you will think of them as nuisances. Their curious nature will led their grubby little paws into everything. Little Aquarians even have quick tempers to try your patience. They can be stubborn and do not seem to appreciate or return your affection. They would rather bite you on the nose than kiss you.

Training the young Aquarian pet will be a test of your patience and ability to forgive. When the topic is interesting to them, they learn fast. But if they are disinterested, you might as well postpone the session. The old adage, "You can lead a horse to water, but you can't make it drink," applies to the easily distracted Aquarian pet.

One way Aquarian pets learn rapidly is by watching another pet in action. They concentrate intently on the new animal and are quick to repeat or mimic the actions. This method of training works especially well for Aquarian hunting dogs, but it will work even for simple house or litterbox training. A well-trained adult pet is an excellent teacher for the young Aquarian, making training proceed much faster.

The Healthy Aquarian

Bones are the Aquarian weak point, so be especially on the watch for

- dislocating knee caps

- arthritis of the knees

- fractures of the lower legs

- ingrown and broken claws

The Aquarian circulatory system can be delicate, too. Blood disorders (anemia, leukemia, bleeding) are not uncommon; watch for frostbite — especially on the tips of the ears in Aquarian cats — and for heartworms in Aquarian dogs.

Aquarian heart problems can include abnormal heart rhythm and rapid heart rates from tachycardia to outright fibrillation.

Sensitive noses in Aquarian pets will cause them to sneeze frequently, and discharges from the nose are common.

Cigarette or cigar smoke is often especially irritating to the Aquarian pet's nose.

Aquarius Summary

If you are a patient and forgiving person, the Aquarian pet will fill your life with interesting and unusual moments. These rascals are a little different. Their independence and originality make their personalities almost comical. They can be a constant source of enjoyment for tolerant owners.

Aquarius Pet Compatibilities

Aquarius pets are an odd bunch. It is often difficult to find suitable companions for these independent and spirited creatures.

Pets of the sun signs Cancer, Libra, and Capricorn are the best housemates for Aquarius pets.

Pets of the signs Aries, Gemini, Scorpio, Sagittarius, Aquarius, and Pisces are best suited as their neighbors or friends.

Taurus, Leo, and Virgo pets should be watched carefully when confronting Aquarius pets.

Aquarius Pets — Aquarius Pets

This is a lively combination, too lively for most owners. When these two are kept outside there are few problems. They will bounce around the yard, to and fro, curious to see what the other has found. When this pair is cooped up inside, their insatiable, inquisitive natures will lead them into all sorts of trouble-causing adventures. Fighting is rare between Aquarian pets.

Aquarius Pets — Pisces Pets

Animals of these sun signs will often run to greet each other when they first meet. Aquarius will be the more active of the two, recognizing an attentive audience in Pisces. Pisces pets and Aquarius pets will spend as much time apart as together. It is not unusual for Aquarius to abandon Pisces in the midst of their play. Owners must be careful not to blame a sensitive Pisces pet for things that could have been done by Aquarius.

Aquarius Pets — Aries Pets

When these sun signs first meet they won't get along at all, but after two or three encounters they will become good friends. The relationship eventually becomes energetic and intense. Aquarius will lead the way, teaching the Aries all sorts of strange behavioral traits. Aquarius will often abandon Aries when they are off somewhere together and Aquarius will come trotting home, apparently pleased to have ditched Aries somewhere. Aquarius pets need time alone and do not do as well in the relationship if they are forcibly housed with Aries.

Aquarius Pets — Taurus Pets

The often pesty Aquarius triggers Taurus's anger. Fights are frequent between these two opposing sun signs. When not fighting, they are indifferent to each other and will growl when one comes near the other. The obedient Taurus pet and the often disobedient Aquarius pet rarely find any neutral turf. This is an explosive match-up.

Aquarius Pets — Gemini Pets

When Gemini and Aquarius pets get together, they are difficult to control. They bring out one another's wild side. You never know what these two will get into. They can destroy a room in a matter of minutes. They have frequent bouts of sparring, make a lot of noise, and generally act like a couple of jumping beans with each other. Gemini and Aquarius will not obey their owners' commands when they are together.

Aquarius Pets — Cancer Pets

Cancer-born pets' tempers flare when their secure homes are invaded by inquisitive Aquarian pets. Cancer pets are constantly scurrying about the house attempting to head Aquarius off at the pass. There are few tender moments between them. Cancer refuses to join in with Aquarius's active and impulsive behavior and Aquarius refuses to be affectionate with Cancer.

Aquarius Pets — Leo Pets

Owners should keep Leo and Aquarius pets separate. Their tempers are short with each other and fierce battling may ensue. Often, only human intervention prevents serious injury. When they first meet, animals of these sun signs seem friendly and fascinated with each other, but sniffing soon turns into biting.

Aquarius Pets — Virgo Pets

The more distance the better between these two pet signs. Fighting is not the problem; the problem is that they bring out the worst in one another. Aquarians get along with most other animals, but not with Virgos. Aquarians will bark or meow endlessly in the presence of Virgos. They will become unresponsive to their owners' requests and even unmanageable. Virgo pets become withdrawn when they are around Aquarius pets. They will retreat into their shell of shyness and may not come out of it for days. A backyard fence will provide the Virgo pet with territorial security from a strange Aquarian neighbor. Virgos will retain their normal personalities as long as there is no direct contact with Aquarius.

Aquarius Pets — Libra Pets

There is never a dull moment in a home that has this match-up of pets. There is never any viciousness between the two, but the relationship will run the gamut from friends to enemies. Aquarius pets are the instigators of activities with Libra pets. However, once their playful antics start, with each other, the Libra pet becomes the dominant one. When they occasionally growl and snarl at each other, Libra usually prevails and then they get along just fine. Libra pets willingly accept the tender, loving actions directed at them by Aquarius pets.

Aquarius Pets — Scorpio Pets

Aquarians and Scorpios are nervous around each other. Each keeps a watchful eye on the other's activities. The unpredictable nature of Aquarius, combined with Scorpio's urge to dominate in confrontations with other animals, makes quarrels frequent. Each fears the other, providing a stalemate of nerves at times. This gives the appearance that the two signs are getting along, but the relationship will not remain quiet for long. Keep their meetings short.

Aquarius Pets — Sagittarius Pets

This pairing of sun signs is occasionally volatile. Especially between dogs and cats of these two signs, fighting occurs. Aquarius pets will become overly enthusiastic when attempting to join in Sagittarius pets' activities. They will follow the Sagittarian like a shadow, often sticking their noses where they aren't wanted. A quick snap by Sagittarius sends Aquarius on its way.

Aquarius Pets — Capricorn Pets

Capricorn pets and Aquarius pets are calm and respectful of each other, although a bit noisy when people or other animals come around. They stay together most of the time and are well mannered in one another's presence. Capricorn is very patient with the aggressiveness shown by inquisitive Aquarius. Aquarius pets constantly poke and prod Capricorns when they are relaxing. Capricorns will let Aquarians know when they want to be left alone, and Aquarius will respect Capricorn's subtle growl or nip.

13

Cool, Calm and Collected:

The
PISCES
Pet

February 19 — March 20

The Pisces Personality

Ruled by the planet Neptune, shy Pisces-born pets are gentle, timid, calm, and tranquil. They are very loving and will return your affection; they love to be pampered and taken care of. In fact, unaggressive Pisceans hate confrontation of any sort.

They will go out of their way to avoid run-ins with mean animals or mean people. Pisces pets are smart; when confronted with losing situations, they have inventive ways of sneaking away smoothly, and are good at concealing their emotions when threatened.

Pisces pets are natural weather barometers. They have a built-in sense of impending bad weather. Their personalities will change when storms, tornadoes, and the like are approaching. They may stay glued to your side or in your lap, or they may take to a favorite secluded space. If you learn to recognize these changes, they can warn you of forthcoming weather problems with astonishing reliability.

Pisces shares with Cancer the ability to sense the emotions of people around them. They change with the moods of their owners.

Reprimanding Pisces pet must be done with the utmost caution. They are very sensitive to verbal and physical abuse. They are easily intimidated by aggressive people or animals and will silently withdraw. Don't be too negative towards your Pisces pets when they do something bad. They can usually sense the displeasure on your part, and will stop cold in their tracks when caught in the act. They will then go off and punish themselves in quiet contemplation. Pisces pets are easily humiliated. You can make them feel worthless and useless if you punish them harshly.

Pisces pets stay cool, calm, and collected in the midst of utter chaos. They know how to stay out of the line of direct fire and are rarely the topic of discussions. Their cooperative nature allows them to become submissive when necessary. Pisces pets mind their own business and lead their own quiet lives. They won't impose on your quieter moments. Pisces does not cause household disruptions.

The temper of Pisces pets, in fact, is almost nonexistent. They are hard to excite to the point of violence. For this reason they do well around active or abusive children. Children have an attraction to Pisces pets which is not always reciprocated. The Pisces pet will, however, tolerate all sorts of roughhousing, even if they don't eagerly join in.

Pisces pets have accurate intuition. They will avoid people who aren't animal lovers. Likewise, they are sensitive and responsive to other gentle, kindhearted creatures. They won't approach strangers in their homes, but they are receptive to loving when invited.

As is the case with Virgo pets, Pisces pets are genuinely compassionate towards the sick, disabled, or handicapped. They are a great source of comfort for people in these situations. If someone should bring a stray animal into your home, Pisces will help you nurture it back to health.

Pisces pets spend most of their time at home. Frequent trips over to the neighbor's house are uncharacteristic. They spend a lot of time by themselves. Roaming or wandering behavior should be discouraged early in their lives. Once they get a taste of it they will travel with all the enthusiasm of Sagittarians. Pisces can live a fulfilling life by staying home.

A quiet, peaceful home environment is best for Pisces pets. Constant noise or disruptions will cause them to become withdrawn and reclusive.

Although content to stay in one place most of their lives, Pisces pets do not develop routines. They may eat at all different hours and want to go outside when you least expect it. They enjoy getting new chew toys, new catnip containers, and new foods. They have good appetites, but usually will eat only the more expensive foods.

Pisces pets have good memories. They will remain cautious of previous adversaries. It is difficult to play tricks on Pisces pets. Nothing surprises them and they seem indifferent to most goings-on.

In order for Pisces pets to perform, you will have to give them much praise for their accomplishments. If they have an appreciative audience, they will even become lively and show off.

You will often find your Pisces cat or dog in the basement or cellar. Pisceans love to explore dark places and very often become active at night.

Pisces-born pets are not very vocal. They don't howl, bark, or meow loudly. They have soft, mellow voices. They do well in apartments because they are quiet and content to stay home.

Most Pisces-born animals are short and small for their breed. They often have large, bulging eyes that are prone to infections and injury. Their fur is soft and fine, sometimes with mild waves running throughout. They have large heads and move around slowly and gracefully. They appear dainty and fragile. They have small teeth and small paws for their body size.

The Pisces Parent

Pisces-born pets make fine parents. They have a special fondness for their weak young, but will not neglect their healthy offspring while taking care of the sick as the Virgo pet parent is prone to do. They are very patient when it comes to nursing the hungry crew, and they keep their young extremely clean. They rarely discipline the little ones, allowing them freedom to wander about and explore. Their litter is usually spread all over the house once the little ones learn to walk.

The Young Pisces

The newborn Pisces pet is often sickly when young. Many have to be surgically removed from their mothers' wombs, and I do a number of Cesarean sections during the Pisces period. They grow strong as the weeks go by. You may think you have picked a loser the first few weeks you have your Pisces youngster, but trips to the veterinarian will become less frequent as they mature. You won't be able to get your Pisces youngster to eat or sleep at regular predictable intervals. Remember: Pisceans just don't develop strong routines.

Young Pisces pets are quiet. It is hard to teach Pisces dogs to "speak." Even Siamese cats, known for their vocalizations, are quieter when Pisces is their sun sign.

Young Pisces pets are timid, and may not venture far from the little box or blanket they consider home. Gentle coaxing on your part will be needed to reassure them. They are very often inattentive to your commands. They will develop their own pace of doing things. Pisces puppies or kittens are manageable if you show them affection and encourage their achievements. Remember, they are sensitive to reprimands. Be tolerant and don't punish them unless it is absolutely warranted. If you treat them cruelly, they will become withdrawn, silent, and untouchable.

The Healthy Pisces

Paw Patrol? For Pisces' sensitive feet, absolutely. They're vulnerable to pododermatitis (infections and inflammation on the paws and between the toes) and, frequently, to itching and chewing of the paws.

Look out, as well, for upper respiratory infections with heavy mucous discharges from the nose, pneumonia in the lungs, and the serious condition known as collapsing trachea, which is signaled by persistent coughing.

Pisces' sensitivities are unusually strong. Reactions to vaccinations bear watching. Observe your little Pisces pet for at least a half hour after it receives a vaccination (or any other injection, such as penicillin). Drug reactions are very rare, but the majority I see are in Pisces-born pets.

Due to the large and protruding eyes of many Pisces pets, injuries, infections, and irritations are frequent.

These tendencies also apply to sensitive Pisces skin. Staph and other infections of the skin, and itching and self-mutilation from chewing, are common in Pisces pets. Look out, too, for neurodermatitis in Pisces cats — a constant licking of the skin, to the point of irritation. In Pisces dogs, the same tendency leads to lick granulomas, when licking and chewing of the lower legs thickens and inflames the skin.

Pisces Summary

If you are looking for a quiet pet, one that will be gentle, loving, and affectionate, Pisces is a good choice. Pisceans do very well in small living quarters or apartments. They do not need to be outdoors for any great lengths of time. They are safe around children, but do equally well without them. They are a comfort to the ill or disabled. You won't be able to be too rough on discipline with the Pisces pet, but they rarely need it.

Pisces Pet Compatibilities

Gentle Pisces pets rarely fight with other dogs or cats. Their sensitive nature allows them to be intimidated easily by aggressive opponents.

Pisces-born pets are most compatible and willing to share their homes with animals of the sun signs Taurus, Gemini, Cancer, Virgo, Scorpio, and Sagittarius.

Animals with the signs of Leo, Libra, Capricorn, Pisces, and Aquarius are more suited to occasional encounters with Pisces pets.

Pisces pets and Aries pets do not complement each other in any way.

Pisces Pets — Pisces Pets

This pairing does best when the pets are opposite sexes or dogs and cats. Two males or two females together make each other lazy. When they are opposite sexes or species they are affectionate toward each other, often pampering one another out of sight of their owners in a secluded or dark area. The home environment will be very quiet and when friends visit your home, they may not even know your two Pisces pets are around.

Pisces Pets — Aries Pets

Pisces pets do not think much of energetic Aries pets. Aries pets are too forward and physical in their advances toward Pisces pets. Aries will be jubilant, bounding, and enthusiastic in greeting Pisces, but this rubs Pisces the wrong way. Pisces never gives in and this causes the usually active Aries to become depressed and quiet. Occasionally Aries pets keep trying to stimulate Pisces pets to action and this results in violently flaring tempers.

Pisces Pets — Taurus Pets

Taurus pets bring Pisces pets to life, often more than quiet Taurus would like. Pisces is the initiator of actions between the two. Taurus rarely approaches Pisces. Pisces is lively around Taurus. Occasionally Taurus will try to interrupt the active little Pisces, but Pisces will resist Taurus's settling influence. There will be plenty of tender and calm moments between the two and Taurus will cherish and dominate these intimacies.

Pisces Pets — Gemini Pets

There is a lot of give and take between Gemini and Pisces. Pisces pets are slow to join in the action with Gemini pets, but they eventually do. Pisces has a soothing and calming effect on Gemini. Gemini will even lie still long enough for Pisces to show affection. Pisces and Gemini will lick, nibble, and roll around with each other in moments uncharacteristically tender for Gemini.

Pisces Pets — Cancer Pets

This pairing of signs will blend harmoniously into most households. Pisces pets are gentle and caressing toward Cancer-born pets. Cancer will allow Pisces to be the protector, although Cancer is the boss between the two. Pisces and Cancer pets will stay indoors and close to home most of the time, and violent moments between them are rare. This combination of animal signs works equally well between dogs and cats.

Pisces Pets — Leo Pets

Leo pets make Pisces pets less inhibited and the two will actively play together. Leo will guard Pisces like a favorite toy. Pisces will be submissive while Leo dominates the relationship. The constant prodding of Pisces by Leo often leads to a rare outburst of Piscean temper. If these two are kept together for extended periods of time, Pisces has a tranquilizing effect on Leo.

Pisces Pets — Virgo Pets

Virgo pets and Pisces pets form happy, docile unions. They are both a bit shy and are compassionate to their owners and to each other. Virgo is usually dominant in this relationship, although not to the point of inhibiting Pisces' personality. Pisces will bring the Virgo pet out of its shyness and they will play together frequently. The play will start out gently and will culminate with playful growling, snarling, and thrashing around. This is usually uncharacteristic for both of these animal signs. They are happy and genuinely relaxed with each other's company. Although the Virgo is usually the dominant one in the Virgo-Pisces pet relationship, Virgo will become more affectionate to humans when a Pisces pet is around.

Pisces Pets — Libra Pets

Pisces and Libra pets are both easygoing and gentle-natured, but they don't get along very well. Pisces' efforts to play and make friends with Libra are usually rejected. Intuitive Pisceans pick up on this rejection and will go off to spend time by themselves. There is even occasional aggressiveness between these two animal signs, uncharacteristic behavior for both. Pisces' astute memory will document Libra's resistance for future encounters.

Pisces Pets — Scorpio Pets

Pisces pets bring out the performer in Scorpios. Scorpios will be physically active around Pisces, but rarely aggressive. Scorpio will even stimulate the normally shy Pisces into joining in the playful antics. Scorpio does not feel the urge to dominate Pisces by fighting. This relationship is relatively quiet when compared to most of Scorpio's animal encounters. Pisces pets are a good influence on Scorpio-born pets, as are Sagittarius pets.

Pisces Pets — Sagittarius Pets

Pisces pets are receptive toward Sagittarius's advances. They eagerly join in the freewheeling activities of Sagittarians and will even become more adventurous. It is not unusual for Pisces to go on an uncharacteristic trip away from home with Sagittarius. Pisces pets are the initiators of tender moments between the two and these moments last but a short time. The abundance of enthusiasm on Sagittarius pets overflows and makes Pisces happier and more active.

Pisces Pets — Capricorn Pets

Capricorn will dominate submissive Pisces. The Pisces pet will be outwardly affectionate toward the Capricorn pet, but Capricorn will not return all of Pisces' licks and nibbles. This pet partnership does best when there are children around to interact with both of them, since Pisces pets do not receive the attention they need from Capricorn pets. When these two signs are kept together in the same house, Capricorn rules the day and Pisces becomes active during the night while Capricorn is sleeping.

Pisces Pets — Aquarius Pets

Animals of these sun signs will often run to greet each other when they first meet. Aquarius will be the more active as Pisces is an attentive audience. Pisces pets and Aquarius pets will spend as much time apart as together. It is not unusual for Aquarius to abandon Pisces in the midst of their playfulness. Owners must be careful not to blame their sensitive Pisces pet for things that could have been done by Aquarius.

14

The Happy, Healthy, New Age Pet

Sharing your family life with a pet is a unique experience. Your pet will progress from infant to juvenile to adult to geriatric within a time frame that produces relatively little change in you. Compassionate understanding of your pet's personality and stage of maturity will be mutually beneficial.

The first thing you must do after acquiring your new pet, young or old, is to establish its *trust* in you and your family. The goal is to minimize *stress* to your newcomer at all costs. Don't worry about any other training until this is accomplished. (The exception is violent, aggressive behavior such as is frequent in Scorpio animals; this must be disciplined immediately.) Trust is developed in the first few days. Start by feeding your pet frequent small meals, regardless of its age (the amount and type of food depends on the pet's age, of course). Have all family members take turns dishing out the food. Your pet will have a positive and happy association with each family member. Another trust-building experience is to give your new pet lots of verbal and physical affection; this is especially needed by Cancer and Taurus pets. Overlook all minor offenses the first few days. Do not mete out punishment unless absolutely necessary, as it may be with Sagittarius and Scorpio pets. If your newly acquired pet is very young, five to seven weeks or so, pamper it no end when it cries or seems confused or frightened. You will not spoil it at this point in its life, even if it is going to be a working dog or a "mouser" cat. Bad experiences at such an impressionable age (such as feeling abandoned) can result in lifelong abnormalities. Conversely, enjoyable experiences assure lifelong benefits to both pet and owner.

117

After your pet is comfortable in its new home, and trusts the other inhabitants, you may begin *training* procedures. Needless to say, different animals (different signs) will require different methods. Some are quick to respond and learn (Aries, Virgo), while some are slow movers and slow learners (Taurus, Capricorn). Some respond best when the opposite sex trains them (Gemini), while others prefer taking commands from the same sex (Aries). Some are easier to train when they have an audience (Virgo and Libra), others do much better one-on-one (Taurus and Scorpio).

An especially important decision is how to *discipline* your pet for improper behavior or unwillingness to respond. This decision should not be made ahead of time, but should be determined by the sensitivity of your pet to reprimands. Some pets are very sensitive to the mildest of verbal reprimands (Taurus, Leo, Virgo, and especially Cancer). For these pets, different degrees (tone and loudness) of voice reprimands are sufficient to make your displeasure known, producing as strong a negative association as does physical punishment in stubborn pets. If verbal abuse has no effect, the next stage in disciplining your pet is to grab the critter by the scruff of the neck and shake it for two to three seconds. This is how pet mothers handle them when they are young and it has deep-rooted significance. You should never use your blunt hand for punishment. *The hand should be an object used for rewarding your pet, not punishment.* In certain situations physical punishment may become necessary. If your pet seriously threatens the well-being of another by attacking, or endangers itself by running into the street, drastic steps must be taken. In order for your pet to associate the dastardly deed with the punishment, be sure your response coincides with or immediately follows the event. Be especially careful not to reprimand with your hand if you are going to use hand signals to train your pet (as with hunting dogs). The only two signs in which some controlled physical reprimands may become necessary are Scorpio (frequently) and Sagittarius (infrequently). Some pets easily learn "tricks" (Virgo and some Libras) while others dislike performing tricks for amusement of their owners (Sagittarius, Scorpio, and most Aquarians).

Some general but important facts about training are helpful to know and remember. The best you can hope for is to modify and control your pet's inherent behavior. You cannot "create" your pet's behavior patterns or responses. Work within its personality and abilities (abilities will progress). Most importantly, work at your animal's pace, not at your own. Give enough time for slow movers and slow learners to respond. Start reprimanding your pet with the mildest of discipline (mild vocal) and increase from that point until your pet shows you a response. Physical punishment is almost never necessary and should be reserved for very serious or life-threatening situations. Some pets (Aquarius) perk right up after being disciplined, while others (Taurus and especially Cancer) stay depressed or seem confused for longer periods. Use discipline sparingly on sensitive pets, overlooking their mistakes but praising them to no end for their accomplishments. Always be more patient and persistent than your trainee. Slow learners and slow movers can usually have longer training sessions than can active, quick, fast-paced youngsters. Keep the training sessions short and frequent for fast-paced, active pets. The slower animals may actually progress ahead of the quicker pets because of the extra time that can be spent with them. *Rewards* for deeds well done should be by voice and physical affection. Food or treats should not be used. All the necessary functions a pet must master to cohabit with humans can be accomplished without bribery with foods. Treats may be necessary to get some reluctant pets to perform tricks (especially Sagittarius).

House training or *litterbox* training is not as difficult as most owners suppose. If your new pup or kitten is very young, say five to six weeks of age, then you should not expect any progress for a couple of weeks. Animals of this young age are unable to retain quantities of urine and have to go frequently, even in their own box if kept in one. Never discipline an animal of this age for not being able to control itself. This does not mean you should not try to help it develop good habits. Take it frequently to the latrine area, every time you remove it from its sleeping quarters. It will improve dramatically as it reaches age eight or nine weeks. At this age it is still best not to discipline your new pet for occasionally urinating where it shouldn't. Discipline usually just causes confusion. One hint for parents is to leave the newly acquired pup or kitten asleep in a box next to your son or daughter's bed at night. Leave instructions with your child to take the new addition to the latrine area if it awakes during the night. Two or three trips during the night is not uncommon and children love seeing the immediate progress and results of their efforts. Keep the pup or kitten confined to its sleeping quarters when you are not there to observe and respond to its whimpers or cries. You can gradually enlarge the area you leave it in when alone. The trick is to get it to understand the entire area that you let it live in is its "home." A dog or cat will not soil its own home.

Regular meals make house training or litterbox training easier than if the food is left out continually. After eating there is a reflex for the animal to "make room for more" so it usually has a bowel movement. Leave the food down for twenty minutes or until it is finished eating, whichever comes first, then take it to the latrine area and *wait*. Usually within five to ten minutes the reflex occurs. Five to ten minutes may seem like hours in the dead of winter, so be patient.

If your animal, pup or kitten, is destructive when you leave it home alone (usually Libra), leaving a full bowl of food and water may prevent its boredom and ease its fear of being confined.

"An old pet," it's been said, "is someone's old friend." In general, small dogs live longer than large dogs (Capricorns may outlive them all). Just the opposite is true of cats. Large cats live longer than small cats. As your pets approach their golden years (as young as six or seven years for some large-breed dogs), you should realize this, and treat them accordingly. Be more tolerant. They are set in their ways and you might as well accept it. Respect them as you would an elder. Accommodating them at this stage of their lives will give you a warm feeling inside once they are memories.

About the Author

Donald Wolf, D.V.M., was a busy Michigan veterinarian for ten years before moving to Wyoming in 1986 to participate in the prestigious federal/state project to save the endangered black-footed ferret, at that time the rarest mammal in North America. He is currently propagating the species in captivity for eventual re-introduction to the wild. (This species, once thought to be extinct, has increased from a low of eighteen in 1986 to a current high of 122, with re-introduction projected for 1991.) In addition, he is a wildlife veterinarian with the Wyoming Game & Fish Department. He has published over a dozen articles in professional journals.